The View from Under My Desk:
My Battle with Depression in the Workplace

Brad Anderson

© Copyright 2019 Beacon Publishing Group
All rights reserved.

No portion of this book may be reproduced in whole or in part, by any means whatsoever, except for passages excerpted for the purposes of review, without the prior written permission of the publisher.

For information, or to order additional copies, please contact:

Beacon Publishing Group
P.O. Box 41573 Charleston, S.C. 29423
800.817.8480| beaconpublishinggroup.com

Publisher's catalog available by request.

ISBN-13: 978-1-949472-68-4

ISBN-10: 1-949472-68-4

Published in 2019. New York, NY 10001.

Printed in the USA.

Advance Praise for <u>The View from Under My Desk</u>

"Brad Anderson gives us a beautifully written, achingly honest first-person account of depression. I recommend this to anyone who is on the inside of depression or on the outside looking in--as a leader, a friend, or a loved one."

Angela Duckworth
Christopher H. Browne Distinguished Professor of Psychology at the University of Pennsylvania and author of The New York Times bestselling book, <u>Grit-The Power of Passion and Perseverance</u>

Reading this book was profoundly beautiful even as my heart was in anguish. Brad's willingness to be vulnerable is a gift to all of us and I was inspired by how he did not give up even in the darkest of moments. His story touches all of us, it busts through the misconceptions about depression and the insights provided are a guide to all of us. This book demands to be read so each of us no matter where we are can get out from under our desks

Teresa Roche, Ph.D.
Former Vice President and Chief Learning Officer, Agilent Technologies

The View from Under My Desk shines an uneasy light on the dark world of depression. Brad's personal and jarring story stands in stark contrast to his countless and laudable professional accomplishments. In providing a helpfully uncomfortable glimpse into the mind of someone battling this unseen demon, this book itself is yet another bold statement of the talent and contribution someone struggling with depression is capable of. Although the book reaffirms there are no easy answers to overcoming this insidious condition, it nonetheless provide meaningful insights and hopeful lessons that can be used to lessen its impact and prevalence at work and elsewhere.

Kim Capps
CEO, InsideOut Development

I've been Brad's friend for a long time. He is the genuine article. He doesn't have a phony bone in his body. I'm as familiar with his life, his accomplishments and his struggles as anyone. I'm in awe, not only of what he has written, but the five-star quality of the writing. It is clean, pure and exactly what is needed to guide any fortunate reader through the book. I'm so grateful he wrote it and grateful for the message that distills from it, which is, that with all Brad has been through and continues to go through…he is still standing.

Bruce Neibaur, *Award Winning Screenwriter and Director*

What a story! Brutally honest and personal. I've known Brad for almost 50 years. I had no idea of the depth of his pain and suffering. His gift for writing provides captivating reading about the

Advance Praise for <u>The View from Under My Desk</u>

"Brad Anderson gives us a beautifully written, achingly honest first-person account of depression. I recommend this to anyone who is on the inside of depression or on the outside looking in--as a leader, a friend, or a loved one."

Angela Duckworth
Christopher H. Browne Distinguished Professor of Psychology at the University of Pennsylvania and author of The New York Times bestselling book, <u>Grit-The Power of Passion and Perseverance</u>

Reading this book was profoundly beautiful even as my heart was in anguish. Brad's willingness to be vulnerable is a gift to all of us and I was inspired by how he did not give up even in the darkest of moments. His story touches all of us, it busts through the misconceptions about depression and the insights provided are a guide to all of us. This book demands to be read so each of us no matter where we are can get out from under our desks

Teresa Roche, Ph.D.
Former Vice President and Chief Learning Officer, Agilent Technologies

The View from Under My Desk shines an uneasy light on the dark world of depression. Brad's personal and jarring story stands in stark contrast to his countless and laudable professional accomplishments. In providing a helpfully uncomfortable glimpse into the mind of someone battling this unseen demon, this book itself is yet another bold statement of the talent and contribution someone struggling with depression is capable of. Although the book reaffirms there are no easy answers to overcoming this insidious condition, it nonetheless provide meaningful insights and hopeful lessons that can be used to lessen its impact and prevalence at work and elsewhere.

Kim Capps
CEO, InsideOut Development

I've been Brad's friend for a long time. He is the genuine article. He doesn't have a phony bone in his body. I'm as familiar with his life, his accomplishments and his struggles as anyone. I'm in awe, not only of what he has written, but the five-star quality of the writing. It is clean, pure and exactly what is needed to guide any fortunate reader through the book. I'm so grateful he wrote it and grateful for the message that distills from it, which is, that with all Brad has been through and continues to go through…he is still standing.

Bruce Neibaur, *Award Winning Screenwriter and Director*

What a story! Brutally honest and personal. I've known Brad for almost 50 years. I had no idea of the depth of his pain and suffering. His gift for writing provides captivating reading about the lengths one might go to find relief from depression. His incredibly successful life is an example of what can be accomplished in spite of debilitating mental illness. He provides hope for us all.

C. Reed Ernstrom, *President / CEO Bear River Mental Health Services, Inc.*

In this book, Brad Anderson provides a remarkably honest and forthright account of his persistent attempts to find relief from treatment-resistant depression. As a masterful storyteller, he brings to life the pain, suffering, struggles and impairment associated with major depressive disorder, which are generally not known nor understood by family, friends and associates. The takeaways from this book include the strategies that he has found helpful in dealing with his depression, which may be of help to others so afflicted. In addition, the narrative will help family, friends, co-workers, supervisors and employers to be more aware of and empathetic towards persons dealing with depression and should be helpful in providing reasonable accommodation for them. Finally, it is my personal hope that this account will be instrumental in reducing the stigma associated with major depressive disorder, thus allowing a more open dialogue and an improved outcome for all involved.

David B. Bylund, Ph.D.
Former President of the American Society for Pharmacology and Experimental Therapeutics

Contents

Foreword	
Chapter 1	Why I Lie Under My Desk
Chapter 2	The Spring from Hell
Chapter 3	Depression: Inherited?
Chapter 4	College Years and Early Self-Medicating
Chapter 5	Transitions
Chapter 6	Frozen with Despair on a Frozen Campus
Chapter 7	Success and Setback in a Startup
Chapter 8	Seven Habits of Highly Effective People
Chapter 9	Don't Abruptly Stop Taking Your Meds
Chapter 10	Jobless and Aimless
Chapter 11	Opiates
Chapter 12	Rudderless

Chapter 13	The Promise of a New Treatment
Chapter 14	Getting a Real Job
Chapter 15	Another Start-up and The Next Miracle Cure
Chapter 16	Electroconvulsive Therapy: Going for the Gold Standard
Chapter 17	Hitting True Rock Bottom
Chapter 18	My $8/hour Gig
Chapter 19	A New Beginning
Chapter 20	How to Avoid Becoming an A-hole Boss and What to do to Survive One
Chapter 21	Current State of Affairs
Chapter 22	Wrapping Up and the Role of the Will in Depression

Foreword

If you suffer from depression, this book is for you. If you are leader who cares about those in your organization who carry this burden, this book is for you. If you are a friend or loved one of someone trying to make it through life with depression, you'll be happy you found Brad Anderson. I fit two of those categories in Brad's life.

In The View from Under My Desk, Brad Anderson confronts leaders—like me—with three jarring questions:

1. *Practical*: How many of my employees are "under their desks"—figuratively or literally? And what is it costing me?
2. *Ethical*: What role am I—or my workplace—playing in amplifying their suffering?
3. *Personal*: Where was I when Brad crawled under his desk?

To be honest, the order of those three was reversed as I read the first draft of my friend's manuscript.

Brad Anderson is a genius. He was *the* driving force behind the meteoric growth of Stephen Covey's 7 Habits of Highly Effective People—turning Stephen's life-changing ideas into a trainable curriculum that touched the lives of tens of millions around the world. He is one of the most creative and effective teachers I have ever met. He is a world-class film producer. He is a careful scholar. He is a remarkable athlete. He is a doting father and grandfather. And he is a loyal friend.

In this book, I belatedly learned how to be a loyal friend for people like Brad. Behind his back my colleagues and I refer to Brad as the "Bob Newhart of the Training Industry." His dry wit coupled with his emotionless delivery triggers delayed reaction laughs that you savor long after a conversation.

As I read Brad's book, I had delayed reactions of a different kind. His story took me back through the thirty years in which I've known Brad. In that time, I have admired, learned from, worked with, and employed him. And I apparently never knew him.

I know now that one day in the 1980s while I sat in a cubicle close enough to him to discern his brand of deodorant I had no clue he was contemplating suicide. I know now that while I was cajoling him into stepping in front of a classroom, I know now, years later I was provoking crippling anxiety. I discovered with regret how the boss I had him report to unintentionally amplified his feelings of powerlessness and despair.

One of Brad's gifts is his unflinching transparency. *The View from Under My Desk* draws you into an abrupt intimacy with this remarkable man in a way that will endow you not just with empathy but also with insight. You'll not only come to understand the work world of those who suffer with depression, but you'll feel more confident in your capacity to relate to, support, and lead those so afflicted in a more *practical, ethical,* and *personal* way.

The implications of this book for leaders, family and friends are profound. This book makes a pathbreaking contribution for leaders who hope to create high-performance organizations in a world where depression is increasingly common. It engages readers in healthy deliberation about their ethical responsibilities to these employees and colleagues.

But for me, its greatest gift was helping me connect more deeply with a beloved friend.

Joseph Grenny
New York Times Bestselling Author of *Crucial Conversations* and *Influencer* and co-founder of VitalSmarts, Inc.

Brad Anderson

Chapter 1: Why I Lie Under My Desk

"When you suffer from depression, 'I'm tired' means a permanent state of exhaustion that sleep doesn't fix." Author unknown

    The title of this book is literal. I occasionally try to escape my depression by lying on the floor of my office, hidden from view by my desk. To the non-depressed, I'm certain this sounds bizarre. What could possibly be gained from putting yourself in this position? I've never spoken to another depressed person about this practice to learn if others use it, but, for me, lying down brings a small amount of relief from depression's hell. Sitting at a desk, or shopping, or taking the car in for repairs, or exercising all require energy. When I'm depressed, I often lack energy, and five minutes lying on the floor offers the briefest of respites from the toil of depressive illness.

    An office I once occupied came with one of those long panes of glass, enabling passersby to easily see me sitting at my desk. So as not to be seen staring up from the desk's underside, I covered the window with flipchart paper that had been used in a meeting, allowing myself to take the prone position when needed. Once, when I was looking for individual office space during a period of unemployment, I was shown several options by the office manager. I recall the surprise on his face when I said, "I want that one," referring to a tiny, closed-in space, with no view of the outside world.

The View from Under My Desk

My current workspace is an enormous room, but I'm its only occupant. The room also functions as a warehouse of sorts, storing stacks of boxes of a book I co-authored. These stacks are situated between the interior window and my desk, so that when I lie down with my legs drawn up in the fetal position, a fellow employee walking by and looking in can't see me. I keep the lights turned out, and frequently lock the door, so that on those rare occasions when someone wants to walk into this room, I have enough time while the person is fiddling with the key to the office to quickly jump up and pretend to have dropped something on the floor. I don't think I've been found out unless someone who works in this small business ever reads of my lying-on-the-floor strategy. The company's lenient dress code also allows me to hide my pillow-matted hair from lying on the floor beneath my golf hat.

This odd habit—lying on the floor of my office looking out from under my desk—is one strategy that has helped me cope with depression in the workplace. I tell my story both to help others understand how depression affects people in the workplace and to offer suggested strategies for dealing with it. Some of the strategies have helped me; some have not, but I think they might help other people; and some might have helped me if I had known about them when I needed them. I've attempted to draw lessons from the strategies I share for lessening depression's impact and prevalence at work.

I've written this book with three separate audiences in mind: those who suffer depression, those who manage people who suffer depression at work, and the coworkers, family and friends of the sufferers. To the depressed, I hope that my story of battling this hellish condition can help to shed a light on that reality which so often goes un-discussed and unacknowledged. I also hope it encourages perseverance in the face of misery, along with a never-ending quest to find help. To leaders, I hope that knowing that a segment of your workforce battles this unseen demon can lead to creating a more depressive friendly organizational culture. I also hope to lessen the stigma attached to mental illness, a stigma that prevents many sufferers from receiving help. And to those in the immediate circle of a depressed individual, I hope that something here can create a bit more understanding of the daily struggles your friend, associate, or loved one endures.

    I've been employed by organizations that proved toxic to my mental health and the suffering has been unrelenting, making my life absolute torture. Unless senior management is actively engaged in creating a mental health friendly culture, organizations can quickly devolve into nightmarish environments for *any* employee, depressed or not. Rogue managers who rule their domains with arrogance, become poisoned by power, clumsily conduct performance reviews, engage in political in-fighting, set unrealistic deadlines and performance targets, and pursue countless other dysfunctional organizational practices can be particularly debilitating to depressives, causing damage to the mental health necessary for organizations to thrive. Depressives *can* be productive, integral members of

The View from Under My Desk

organizations, making valuable contributions enabling the organization to achieve its vision, mission and purpose. My experience is there is much leaders can do to create and sustain depression-friendly cultures.

    To be clear, I am not a therapist, psychologist, licensed clinical social worker, doctor, or psychiatrist. It is not my intention for readers to attempt to practice therapy—that's best left to the professionals. However, I believe that leaders and coworkers can gain increased insight into the struggles of depressives, and if nothing else, become more inclusive of them as you go about your daily routine, as loneliness is a battle many depressed individuals create for themselves by withdrawing socially. Conventional wisdom holds that its best to leave a depressed person alone. Since depression is a disease of loneliness, this turns out to be well-intended but false advice. For those that suffer, my hope is that you might see some of yourself in the battles I've fought and resolve, to the extent possible, to keep the fight alive, difficult as that might be in the worst of times. There is no one size fits all in reducing the pain of depression. As Andrew Solomon states, *"People are discouraged by the news that every case of depression is different from all others, that what works for one person will fail for the next. But that unwelcome reality is the truth of the matter."* The encouraging news is that effective treatments do exist for all but the most stubborn cases of depression.

Signs and Symptoms

Here are some of the more obvious signs that can be detected through words or nonverbal behavior that can signal the presence of depression. This list is not exhaustive, and the prevalence of each sign or symptom is merely a potential indication. The key is to notice when these behaviors vary from a person's typical personality and persist for a period of two weeks or more.

For the depressed, the signs and symptoms are all too familiar. For those seeking to better understand what to look for, whether you're a manager or a concerned coworker, friend or loved one, here's a list of common behaviors that may reflect a depressive episode. A person suffering depression often:

• Appears to be persistently sad and anxious
• Expresses feelings of hopelessness or pessimism
• Expresses feelings of guilt, worthlessness, or helplessness
• Is irritable and restless
• Shows a loss of interest in things that used to be pleasurable, a condition known as anhedonia, after its root, hedonic, which means to experience pleasure
• Withdraws from social interaction
• Experiences formerly routine tasks as burdensome and takes longer to complete them
• Readily quits or gives up on tasks or assignments when faced with opposition or difficulty

The View from Under My Desk

- Becomes angry or hostile (particularly in men)
- Appears to experience stress more than in the past
- Has difficulty making decisions
- Finds it hard to concentrate
- Experiences a decrease in energy and battles fatigue on a daily basis
- Expresses a depressed mood

This book is a sometimes raw look at a life informed by a treatment-resistant mental illness. I have held nothing back. I've tried to share my foibles, my triumphs, my failures with treatments, and those things that have been helpful. On several occasions, I've questioned my sanity in putting this story out there—I've shared my struggles with depression with a small number of people and do my best to hide this reality I live with in my everyday affairs. Memorializing my depression in a book is a huge leap into the arena of vulnerability. I do so in the hope that it might be of some value to fellow sufferers and those that manage them at work.

I've read four memoirs of depression, each written by talented authors—I highly recommend them for additional insights. One is *The Noonday Demon* by Andrew Solomon, a landmark in its genre. The book is part memoir, part an exhaustive discussion of just about every facet of the disease. Another is William Stryon's short and brilliantly crafted *Darkness Visible,* which I read many years ago as my depression worsened. I came across another while doing research for this book and found it to be an easy read with many recommendations for coping with depression. It's called *Shoot the Damn*

Signs and Symptoms

Here are some of the more obvious signs that can be detected through words or nonverbal behavior that can signal the presence of depression. This list is not exhaustive, and the prevalence of each sign or symptom is merely a potential indication. The key is to notice when these behaviors vary from a person's typical personality and persist for a period of two weeks or more.

For the depressed, the signs and symptoms are all too familiar. For those seeking to better understand what to look for, whether you're a manager or a concerned coworker, friend or loved one, here's a list of common behaviors that may reflect a depressive episode. A person suffering depression often:

- Appears to be persistently sad and anxious
- Expresses feelings of hopelessness or pessimism
- Expresses feelings of guilt, worthlessness, or helplessness
- Is irritable and restless
- Shows a loss of interest in things that used to be pleasurable, a condition known as anhedonia, after its root, hedonic, which means to experience pleasure
- Withdraws from social interaction
- Experiences formerly routine tasks as burdensome and takes longer to complete them
- Readily quits or gives up on tasks or assignments when faced with opposition or difficulty

The View from Under My Desk

- Becomes angry or hostile (particularly in men)
- Appears to experience stress more than in the past
- Has difficulty making decisions
- Finds it hard to concentrate
- Experiences a decrease in energy and battles fatigue on a daily basis
- Expresses a depressed mood

    This book is a sometimes raw look at a life informed by a treatment-resistant mental illness. I have held nothing back. I've tried to share my foibles, my triumphs, my failures with treatments, and those things that have been helpful. On several occasions, I've questioned my sanity in putting this story out there—I've shared my struggles with depression with a small number of people and do my best to hide this reality I live with in my everyday affairs. Memorializing my depression in a book is a huge leap into the arena of vulnerability. I do so in the hope that it might be of some value to fellow sufferers and those that manage them at work.

    I've read four memoirs of depression, each written by talented authors—I highly recommend them for additional insights. One is *The Noonday Demon* by Andrew Solomon, a landmark in its genre. The book is part memoir, part an exhaustive discussion of just about every facet of the disease. Another is William Stryon's short and brilliantly crafted *Darkness Visible,* which I read many years ago as my depression worsened. I came across another while doing research for this book and found it to be an easy read with many recommendations for coping with depression. It's called *Shoot the Damn*

Dog, by Sally Brampton. The fourth is *An Unquiet Mind*, by Kay Redfield Jamison.

Each author is eloquent in his or her own ways in discussing the horrors of the disease. And these authors share something in common that differs from my experience: they were healed from the illness. Solomon found relief through a cocktail of medications, along with therapy. Frustratingly, Styron, author of *Sophie's Choice* and other acclaimed novels, offers his readers no insights into his treatment while in hospital that led to his healing. In Brampton's case, she appears to have obtained her once lost mental health through the connections she made with other people, her unwavering desire to resume her role as mother to her young daughter, and therapy. And to be clear, Redfield Jamison suffered from bi-polar disorder, once known as manic-depressive disease, implying it has a depressive component, and differs from what is called unipolar depression with its manic phase requiring different treatment modalities. She was prescribed lithium and went on to become a much sought-after expert in the field of psychiatry.

I envy these writers. I have been declared treatment resistant, having tried just about every psychiatric tool of the trade, all to no avail. I haven't been hospitalized, as were Styron and Brampton, but have seen more than my share of psychiatrists and therapists over the course of many years–more years than I care to remember. I've been a patient of my current psychiatrist for four years, a kind, smart, responsive, creative and compassionate man young enough to be one of my children. I had been seeing him for several months, and everything he tried, including a controversial (at the time) series of ketamine injections, failed to grant me any relief. After discussing one of the most troubling aspects of my depression, the crushing fatigue that felt like life had been sucked out of me, and considering my history of failed treatments, he prescribed the stimulant, Adderall, a drug commonly used for ADHD. My initial response felt like a Godsend. I had energy, my mood was lifted, and I was getting things done. But over the years, my body has adapted to it, and any illusions that this was the miracle cure I'd been seeking all those years came to an end. It helps me achieve a level of functionality I would lack without it, but I still, at times, wind up on the floor or couch, wondering how I'll make it to bedtime. Adderall, as I'll discuss, is no cure all, and comes with its share of unpleasant and likely side effects. I won't list them all but will note just a few. These include anxiety, insomnia, becoming easily angered or annoyed, increased blood pressure, constipation or diarrhea, and one of the most troubling of all: the potential for abuse and addiction. If a doctor or psychiatrist recommends this medication for depression, *please* research all the side effects before using it. I want to state in the strongest way that I am *not* recommending Adderall as a treatment for depression. Adopt the attitude of *caveat emptor* (buyer beware) as you do your own due diligence on the drug. I would love to be Adderall-free; however, it would be disingenuous for me to not mention it.

To underscore the seriousness of depression, consider these grim facts about this condition offered by the World Health Organization and other entities concerned with mental health:

• Globally, over 350 million people of all ages suffer from depression.
• Nineteen percent of Americans will suffer from depression at some time during their lives.
• Eighty percent of depressed people are impaired in their daily functioning.
• Depressed people lose 5.6 hours of productive work every week.
• Productivity is impaired due to a lessened ability to concentrate, lower efficiency, and lessened ability to organize work.
• Depression is the leading cause of disability worldwide, resulting in almost 400 million disability days per year, substantially more than other physical and mental conditions.
• Depression is a major contributor to the global burden of disease.
• More women are affected by depression than men.
• At its worst, depression can lead to suicide.
• There is one death by suicide in the U.S. every 13 minutes. (CDC)
• Suicide takes the lives of over 45,000 Americans every year. (CDC)
• Ninety percent of all people who die by suicide have a diagnosable psychiatric disorder at the time of their death.
• Men are four times more likely to complete a suicide attempt than women.

The View from Under My Desk

Please note: Having suicidal thoughts is a symptom of depression. There are resources available for anyone contemplating suicide. The phone number for the National Suicide Lifeline is 1-800-273-8255. Other resources include immediately going to the nearest emergency room as well as seeking professional help from a mental health professional, such as a therapist, a psychiatrist or a licensed clinical social worker.

• Only half of all Americans experiencing an episode of major depression receive treatment.
• Depression is most prevalent in people ages 45-64.

• Men are more likely to try to self-medicate with drugs or alcohol, whereas women are more likely to seek help from friends and family or psychiatrists.
• Depending on the number and severity of symptoms, a depressive episode can be categorized as mild, moderate, or severe.
• In a typical depressive episode, the person experiences depressed mood, loss of interest and enjoyment, and reduced energy leading to diminished activity for at least two weeks.
• Many people with depression also suffer from anxiety symptoms, disturbed sleep and appetite and may have feelings of guilt or low self-worth, poor concentration and even medically unexplained symptoms.
• An individual with a mild depressive episode will have some difficulty in continuing with

ordinary work and social activities but will probably not cease to function completely.
- During a severe depressive episode, it is very unlikely that the sufferer will be able to continue with social, work, or domestic activities, except to a very limited extent.
- There are effective treatments for depression.

    I haven't found that last bullet point to be 100% true. I do receive some benefit from Adderall, which helps alleviate the severe fatigue that often accompanies depression. However, I know that many sufferers find relief in talk therapy, particularly cognitive behavior therapy, or CBT, medication, or a combination of both.
    The biggest downside as I've progressed with putting this book out is my reluctance to go public with such a personal issue—especially one that's seen by the vast majority of people as a character flaw—in other words, the biggest downside to publishing this book is fear. As mentioned, I've told very few people I struggle with depression. To my surprise, since writing this book, I've found myself telling close friends my darkest secret. So far, no one's flinched, but I haven't gone public beyond a small circle. Yet, if one of my superiors sees this, the word is out. I don't see myself as an extrovert, so revealing the things I reveal in this book didn't come easy. I've lain awake many nights, asking myself if I really want to share these stories with those who might come into contact with them. My friends and close colleagues have encouraged me to go forward, having convinced me that if the material in this book

helps just one person, it will have been worth the effort. In a sense, what I've tried to do with this book is show up, and take some comfort from this quote, "The willingness to show up changes us, It makes us a little braver each time . . . courage starts with showing up and letting ourselves be seen." (Brené Brown, *Daring Greatly: How the Courage to Be Vulnerable Transforms the Way We Live, Love, Parent, and Lead)*

    I believe this is what I've experienced, and in that showing up, I have indeed become a little braver in sharing this heretofore hidden aspect of myself.

    I've written this book with the hope that it will somehow provide the spark for a depressive to soldier on and not give up. I also hope supervisors, managers, executives and team members gain an awareness that there are depressives among them and will consider the strategies I've outlined. If these things can occur, baring my soul through these pages in often unflattering ways will have been worth the effort to get out from under my desk and resume typing.

Chapter 2: The Spring from Hell

"April is the cruelest month." T.S. Eliot

During the early spring of 1992, in an all-day executive committee meeting at The Covey Leadership Center, the organization that brought the world the all-time best-selling book in its category, *The Seven Habits of Highly Effective People*, I found myself so overcome with crippling despair for seemingly no reason that I was barely able to speak and function. When it came time for my report, all I could manage was to pop a VHS cassette into a machine and show the group a rough cut of a short film I'd recently produced about trust. That was it. I managed to mumble a few words about the film and quickly sat down, hoping for no questions or feedback from a team that loved to weigh in with their opinions. I was shocked when their only response was spontaneous applause and I felt relieved to have gotten by with so little effort.

Years later, I would come across a quote by Andrew Solomon that summed up this depressive episode which engulfed me: *"Part of what is most horrendous about depression, and particularly about anxiety and panic, is that it does not involve volition: feelings happen to you for absolutely no reason at all."* Pg. 225, The Noonday Demon: An Atlas of Depression. In his popular TED talk, Depression—The Secret We Share, Solomon also avers *"depression is the result of a genetic vulnerability that is evenly distributed among the population and triggering circumstances."* Since there were no

The View from Under My Desk

triggering circumstances in my life at this time, the agony I felt had descended upon me without volition and without reason, rendering me partially paralyzed and in immense emotional pain.

During this time, my work life couldn't have been more rewarding. I had a generous compensation package, was well respected—at least that's my impression—had been given ownership in the company, had all the autonomy I wanted, and was just beginning to produce a series of what would become award-winning short films on leadership. In addition, my home life was stable and happy. I had five active, thriving children and I was heavily involved in their lives, coaching several of their sports teams. From the outside, I'm sure it looked like I had it all. But in spite of appearances, I was dying inside. I recall thinking that something awful must have happened to me as a child, and was now resurfacing, but no memories of anything traumatic came to mind.

As I look back on that time, the great irony was that I was bringing the business world the much acclaimed *Seven Habits of Highly Effective People*, in the form of the seminar I'd created and the best-selling book I'd help bring to fruition. Yet those seven habits didn't make a dent in my increasingly worsened state. It's hard to be proactive—Habit 1—when you've curled up in a ball behind your desk with the door locked, with a note proclaiming you're in an important meeting and not to be disturbed.

Brad Anderson

"Suicidal Ideation"

The period of late winter and early spring that year would prove to be hellish; I recall asking Covey's younger brother, John, a kind and unassuming man ten to fifteen years my senior, who worked at the firm, to allow me to confidentially share my experiences with the crushing misery I was encountering more and more as that winter gave way to spring. The pain was unrelenting, and I felt I needed to tell someone what was going on. I confided to John that I wanted to kill myself—that the pain was becoming unbearable. He did his best to talk me out of suicide, subsequently writing a lengthy, compassionate, handwritten letter to me about my value as a human being, along with the pain a suicide would cause my family, but the condition would remain for several more weeks. Years later, I would learn that psychiatrists and other mental health professionals have a term for what I was expressing to John that day—they call it "suicidal ideation."

It's been said that *"April is the cruelest month,"* the first line of a T.S. Eliot poem, which some believe reflects the great poet's struggles with depression. Conventional wisdom holds that *"suicides are most prevalent during winter months, with the notion that lonely people become despondent during the holidays and take their lives. However, suicides peak during the month of May. Some experts say people can chalk up their depression to the winter blues during darker months. However, when spring arrives, and their spirits do not lift, those who are still depressed must confront*

The View from Under My Desk

their unhappiness. Other experts say that the increase in sunshine, which brings a natural energy boost, gives depressed individuals the drive to end their lives." I am writing this on April 20 and am experiencing some of the worst depression in my life. I hope to make it past May.

In the depths of the disease, the Pulitzer Prize winning novelist, William Styron, known for his work, *Sophie's Choice*, among many other acclaimed novels, wrote in his memoir, *Darkness Visible*, words that ring true for me: *"In depression this faith in deliverance, in ultimate restoration, is absent. The pain is unrelenting, and what makes the condition intolerable is the foreknowledge that no remedy will come- not in a day, an hour, a month, or a minute. If there is mild relief, one knows that it is only temporary; more pain will follow. It is hopelessness even more than pain that crushes the soul. So the decision-making of daily life involves not, as in normal affairs, shifting from one annoying situation to another less annoying- or from discomfort to relative comfort, or from boredom to activity- but moving from pain to pain. One does not abandon, even briefly, one's bed of nails, but is attached to it wherever one goes."*

All of this was happening at the peak of my power and influence in the organization, so I couldn't attribute my depressed state to job woes. I was literally paralyzed. I would close my office door and stare into space, infused with a pain that seemed to have no origin, but was nonetheless debilitating. On two occasions, people walked into my office, took one look at me and asked what was wrong. I had the flu, I lied. I wasn't hiding the pain very well. I had all the autonomy I could have asked for—no one was breathing down my neck, asking for what I'd contributed lately. As mentioned, I enjoyed a substantial compensation package, was deep into developing Seven Habits 2.0, was producing short films by traveling the globe, and had the job world by the tail.

Proposing an Audacious Plan

Seven years prior to the executive committee meeting that I've described, and experiencing no depressive symptoms I can recall, I had approached Covey and the CEO of his new six-person company with an audacious plan, which, to my amazement, they bought. On April Fool's Day 1985, I embarked on one of the most passionate roles of my life: to mold Covey's embryonic concepts centered around becoming more effective at work and at home, into a corporate training curriculum that would eventually affect the lives of millions. I was brimming with confidence and enthusiasm, and despite my limited experience, had no doubts about my ability to pull off the daring plan I'll describe. One characteristic of depression, at least as I experience it today, is to sap my self-confidence. This diffidence often results in making even insignificant decisions arduous. Such was not the case in those days when anything seemed possible.

What I was presuming to do with Covey's *Seven Habits* was to mold some ideas that had been recorded from a speech by Covey in a high school auditorium, which was packaged to constitute a three-cassette audio set that sold for $29.99. From these humble beginnings I went on to develop a three-day training course and a two-day train-the-trainer program that would play a large part in the company's financial success. Most Fortune 1000 companies and countless other organizations across the globe have implemented the program.

Without knowing much about me, this CEO said yes. Yes, he would back me in my dream of creating what was to become the most popular and influential corporate training program ever. I was hired on at around $40 thousand dollars per year, was shown to a space in an open office arrangement and was given a demonstration of the rudiments of operating a Compaq PC. I then proceeded to interview Stephen at length over the course of that summer to outline a six-day video shoot where he would unload all the content from the *Seven Habits* outline we produced. The transcript from the subsequent video become an important component for writing his blockbuster book.

Achieving a Small Win

Looking back on those heady times, I'm struck with the enormity of what I had undertaken. In the early days of the project, I had a staff of one: myself. Yet what enabled me to make slow but steady progress can be understood using a framework that I didn't consciously understand at the time, but now recognize as the embodiment of what a highly regarded organizational psychologist,

Dr. Karl Weick, discovered in his research into the ways organizations approach solving large scale problems. Let me attempt to illustrate how Weick's concept of achieving what he calls small wins enabled me to avoid despair and a sense of being overwhelmed, leading to the successful completion of a project that would take just under two years to bring to market. I should add that as the project progressed, I received invaluable collaboration and support from people I never envisioned entering the picture. Without their commitment and talents, I'd never have been able to produce a finished product.

    I needed frequent face-to-face meetings with Stephen, yet his increasing popularity as a speaker meant he was on the road a good deal of the time, hindering my ability to meet with him to put together the script for the upcoming video shoot. As the reality of his inaccessibility became clear, a simple idea, a small win, led me to a solution. The Salt Lake City airport, from which Stephen departed for his speaking engagements, is a one-hour drive from his home. Why not offer to drive him to the airport, interviewing him on the way, then making notes of our meeting before returning to the office? I still recall that first foray into chauffeuring. It was a chilly morning, and as I knocked on his door to pick him up, I learned that he either thought me to be very poor, or alternatively, possessed scant knowledge of standard equipment in automobiles, asking if my car had a heater, and if not, thoughtfully offering to bring blankets for the both of us. Without knowing it had a name, I was about to achieve my first small

The View from Under My Desk

win, energizing me and generating momentum to create the next shuttle run and the next small win.

Weick's research has shown that individuals, teams, and organizations that bite off too big a problem are setting themselves up for disappointment and frustration. I had not thought through the details I would need to attend to if I were to pull off my grand plan, and disappointment and frustration would have become my unwelcome companions had I not found this unconventional way of meeting with Dr. Covey. Here's what Weick has to say about the value of achieving small wins: *"Attaining even one small win can create the feeling that you are in control of something; this can reduce feelings of hopelessness and helplessness."* There are three words in that quote that connect directly to depression— and my airport drives constituted small wins that kept me from spiraling. Feelings of *hopelessness* and *helplessness* and the sense that events are out of *control* are symptomatic of depression. The simple act of making those airport runs propelled me forward and kept me energized to forge ahead toward the eventual completion of this gigantic (to me) project.

As I look back on those seemingly insignificant drives, I resonate with Weick's definition of small wins: *"a concrete, complete, implemented outcome of moderate importance. By itself, one small win may seem unimportant. A series of small wins at small but significant tasks, however, reveals a pattern that may attract allies, deter opponents, and lower resistance to subsequent proposals. Small wins are controllable opportunities that produce visible results. Once a small win has been accomplished, forces are set in motion that favor another small win. Small wins bring about noticeable and typically successful changes."* Weick's words ring true for the airport shuttle service I was conducting. The simple act of taking advantage of that time with Covey created momentum that brought me that much closer to a finished script.

For the record, based on a series of small wins, unexpected allies appeared on the scene, enabling me to successfully complete the program and begin offering it for sale to organizations large and small.

Seeking Help

By early 1986, I was named a vice president at the tender age of 32 and was on the fast track. But somewhere along the line in '87, with my new program achieving success after success, for seemingly no good reason, and with no precipitating event to trigger it, I mentally devised a suicide plan. I don't recall experiencing depression during this frenetic time at work and home, which makes mentally creating a plan to kill myself perplexing. The plan was to take my Browning .20-gauge semi-automatic shotgun, break it down into two pieces to fit into a large backpack, get on my new mountain bike, ride up Provo canyon, and do myself in. I've since given the two guns I own to a friend to be locked up in one of his four-gun vaults. The reason I gave for asking him to store my guns was that I had

The View from Under My Desk

grandkids visiting me frequently and wanted to protect them. But the real reason was to lessen the chances that I'd use one of my firearms to commit self-destruction.

    The 1987 suicide plan receded in my memory and I gave it very little, if any, thought in the ensuing years. Strangely, I didn't find it troubling. I first knew something was possibly wrong the next year when I took a pain killer and my wife remarked that I seemed happier and easier to be around. As a result of my obviously improved mood, I approached a dentist friend to ask for a prescription of Lortab, but when I took them, I became less able to focus and nausea set in. Self-medicating depression would occur many years later, with disastrous results.

    So I forgot about that pain-killer strategy and went back to being mildly but functionally depressed. Around that time, Prozac was introduced to the world and a friend from out of state was staying at my house. I naively snuck one, thinking that it would offer some relief. It didn't. I would later learn that these drugs, if they are to work at all, can take from four to six weeks to kick in. Then I wrenched my back-playing basketball and was in so much pain I went to see an orthopedic specialist. He ordered x-rays, but nothing showed up, so he gave me a prescription for some muscle relaxers. I was on my way to give a *Seven Habits* presentation in Bend, Oregon, and recall how I looked forward to taking the next pill. So here was yet another experience with a mood-altering drug that tempered my nascent depression.

    By 1990, I began to experience enough

emotional pain that I went to my family doctor, actually his PA, or physician's assistant, and asked for a prescription of Prozac. Eli Lily had done an amazing job of convincing America that relief from all unhappiness is as close as your pharmacy. My symptoms were still mild, and at the time, my job had stalemated. I recall being terrified that the HR department would get a report from the insurance company pointing out my Prozac prescription, fearing the stigma that would cause, a stigma that continues today. Society is slightly more enlightened about mental illness than it was, but many continue to view depression as a character flaw, a weakness that needs to be overcome by sheer force of will, rather than the disease it is. A recent study found that 54% of the population considers depression to be the result of a personal weakness. I took a 10 mg capsule every day and seemed to experience some relief, but in hindsight, a more interesting job assignment was probably more helpful than the drug, which I discontinued after about a year. I've since tried various other antidepressants, each time to no avail.

The Stigma of Depression

When a depression sufferer recognizes he or she needs help, that individual is often confronted by an obstacle not encountered by those seeking relief from physical ailments. That obstacle is the stigma attached to mental illness. I believe this writer, who quotes another writer, gets it right when referring to the stigmatizing of depression. Diana Spechler wrote a series of articles about her own battles with mental

The View from Under My Desk

illness for *The New York Times*. In a piece ironically titled *Seven Thoughts from a Chronically Unhappy Person*, she quotes from a similarly ironically titled article in the Huffington Post. "I often teach about happiness," Tamara Star wrote in "7 Habits of Chronically Unhappy People" for the *Post* last fall. According to Star, life is hard only if you make yourself its victim; happy people "take responsibility for how they got themselves into a mess and focus on getting themselves out of it as soon as possible." Her list includes "Your default belief is that life is hard" and "you concentrate on what's wrong in this world versus what's right.

Spechler continues, "It's a not-so-subtle assertion: Depressed people should just stop being so depressed already. . . I don't mean to single Star out; her piece reflects a widespread attitude — that depression is a failure of will." And later in the article, Spechler refers to an email she received from someone who had read one of her columns: "Why don't you get out there and help others?" a reader emailed me recently in response to an essay I wrote for this series, "and stop thinking so much about yourself?"

I wonder if anyone has ever felt better, or felt motivated to feel better, after receiving messages like these." I'll answer that one. No.

Chapter 3: Depression: Inherited?

"I was not born to be happy, joyous, free. If my body had its druthers, I'd be depressed all the time." Tina Sonego

I believe depression is a biologically inherited disease, and there's plenty of scientific research to show that mental illness is a family illness. Solomon has noted that *"depression is the result of a genetic vulnerability, which is evenly distributed throughout the population, and triggering circumstances."* (from his TED Talk: *Depression, The Secret We Share*). In my case, it seems I likely inherited this genetic vulnerability from my mother. Here's her sad story—one I'm trying desperately to avoid living myself.

    I was a junior in college when my parents divorced. I had grown up in the small university town of Logan, Utah, and my father had managed an independently owned drug/hardware/housewares/photo supplies store—think of a mini Walmart. During my senior year in high school, it was announced that a large chain store was moving to town. My father saw the writing on the wall, that the new store would gut his business with their greater buying power, and he found an opportunity to co-own and build a new store in Sun Valley, Idaho: a sexy, upscale ski resort for the rich and beautiful people who've discovered the pleasures to be found there.

    Prior to making this move, my parents' marriage was coming undone. My bedroom was situated next to the kitchen, and I would awake each morning to the sounds of acrimony being exchanged between my parents. I'm quite certain they weren't aware their voices carried into my bedroom, but they did, and I found their constant arguing to be upsetting. I told a friend at high school that I thought my parents would divorce—a rare and socially frowned upon practice in the local community.

My Family Unravels

Sun Valley is not known for its emphasis on family values, which exacerbated the struggles my family faced, as new challenges had to be dealt with, like locating a place to live, finding new friends, adapting to a new culture that placed a heavy emphasis on partying, and getting my father's new business off the ground. In this environment that seemed to lack rules of any type, my younger siblings had begun sneaking out of the house at night, and the family was coming undone at a rapid rate. As a 17-year old high school senior, I stayed behind in Logan with my grandmother, so I could continue my pursuit of a golf scholarship, which I eventually obtained at Utah State University. But while I was golfing, working, and hanging out with my girlfriend, my parents already shaky marriage foundered amidst this world-class ski resort, made even more difficult with the struggles to establish a new business in a foreign place with foreign values. My five younger siblings suffered through the transition, acting out in ways their new friends introduced them to.

Living in another state and being caught up in my own life, I was spared much of the chaos of my displaced family. But during my infrequent visits to The Valley, it struck me as odd that my father would frequently be the center of attention at various watering holes in the Valley, as he would gather his new friends and key employees and always picked up the tab. My mother was nowhere in sight. As I would later learn, she was developing a drinking problem trying to cope with raising a family in an unfamiliar environment, with no friends and battling her worsening depression. An unhappy marriage was also playing a significant role in my mother's pain.

Genetic Vulnerability and Triggering Circumstances Collide

As mentioned, Utah State University is in Logan, my family's prior home. After the divorce, my mother took my two youngest brothers and moved back there as a disgraced former socialite, suddenly shunned by the very "friends" she'd hobnobbed with during all those years of gaiety of dance clubs, golfing in the ladies league, as my parent's led their lives in the fast lane. They'd been regulars in the country club scene—my father was president of the club at one point. The parties there were booze fests and my parents frequently hosted their own gatherings at our house, the liquor being stored behind a unique bar my father had built that consisted of silver dollars inlaid into the countertop. The social shunning my mother experienced

The View from Under My Desk

following the divorce must have been devastating, since she had once been the center of attention.

At the start of my junior year in college, I moved in with her in an effort to keep living costs down, since my scholarship only covered tuition. I was a self-absorbed 20-year old college student, oblivious to her painful emotional state and the intense loneliness she must have felt.

During Christmas break, I was out with a friend one evening shooting pool and drinking beer at a local watering hole. After a few games of billiards, my friend, who was of legal age, suggested we head out to another bar, The Cactus Club, with a nasty reputation for busting under-aged customers, though I possessed a fake ID. I was 20 but looked more like a fifteen-year-old, which practically guaranteed my arrest if the place got raided by the cops. Nothing scared me more than the thought of landing in jail for being in the wrong place at the wrong age and I declined my friend's invitation and said I was tired and headed home. It would turn out to be a crucial decision.

My mother's house had a strange floor plan: as you walked from the garage into the house, you stepped directly into my bedroom. As I entered my room and turned on the light, I was met by the sight of my mother lying unconscious on the floor, a pool of vomit surrounding her face. The next several minutes were a blur. I have no memory of what went through my mind other than figuring out I had to immediately get her to an emergency room.

What I do recall was figuring out I was

confronted with a crisis. My mother was small, probably weighing no more than 100 pounds. Lifting an unconscious person, even one as light as my mother, took tremendous effort—I quickly learned that an unconscious person is useless in your efforts to move him or her. I hoisted her onto my shoulder, opened the garage door, and got her situated in the back seat of my car, a yellow 1970 VW beetle.

    I'm amazed to this day that I have no recollection of my thoughts during my drive to and from the ER, where I deposited my mother, where her stomach was pumped, and she survived. Maybe I was in shock, but I don't know for certain. No one at the hospital thought to wonder: this kid has been through trauma and should probably see a counselor, since his mother just tried to kill herself and he found her and brought her in. But it was a less enlightened time. So I did the only thing that came to mind, which was to simply return home.

    After cleaning up the vomit, the gravity of the situation began to descend on me. I found an empty bottle of Quaaludes, a powerful sedative that my mother had been prescribed after a hysterectomy. There's a good chance she'd washed them down with some booze, although that's speculation on my part. What I've since learned about the drug is that it has been banned and has no approved medical use. I have no idea how many pills my mother had taken in her unsuccessful suicide attempt, but clearly enough to cause unconsciousness and possibly death. Had I not declined further beer consumption with my friend at the billiards joint that night, the doctors in the ER may not have been able to save her life.

The View from Under My Desk

   The next morning, I was off to my part-time job in a ski shop, and later that day drove to the hospital to fetch my mother. She said nothing about her actions from the night before and I didn't inquire. Nothing was ever said about her suicide attempt in the ensuing years, and it would be decades before I shared it with any of my siblings.
   Suicide is seen by many as a cowardly act, the easy way out. I couldn't disagree more. My mother was experiencing biologically based depression and was driven to her desperate act by that biology coupled with the absolute rejection she experienced from the divorce and displacement. Today, as a 62-year old adult, I feel shame and embarrassment at not having had more empathy for her plight. Fast-forwarding twenty-seven years from that night in the ER, she finally achieved her goal and ended her battle by succumbing to a cocktail of prescription drugs, freely administered by her psychiatrist, with unlimited refills of Xanax and other powerful, addictive, and ultimately deadly pharmaceuticals.
   Thoughts of the demise of the actor Robin Williams and the method he used are occasionally in the back of my mind. His death was neither cowardly nor thoughtless toward his loved ones as some pundits have claimed, but a rational response to unbearable pain, as are the approximately 45,000 suicides that take place in the United States each year, with ninety percent having a mood disorder as their cause. I agree with this quote from Sally Brampton, *"Wanting to die (or suicidal ideation' as the experts would have it) goes hand in hand with*

the illness. It is a symptom of severe depression, not a character failing or moral flaw. Nor is it, truly, a desire to die so much as a fervent wish not to go on living. All depressives understand that distinction." I now understand that distinction but would possess no inkling at the time that I possessed the same depressive biology as my mother. Nor would I know that this inherited tendency would one day lead me to concoct a suicide plan.

Parenting and Depression

As strong as the biological connection for developing depression has proven to be, the behavioral impact of being raised by depressed parents cannot be overlooked. I found this paragraph on the impact of parental discord upon children in Sally Brampton's book: *"A study by E. Mark Cummings, a professor of psychology at the University of Notre Dame, Indiana, examined the impact of parental conflict on children's future behavior. It found that the manner in which parents handle everyday marital conflicts has a significant effect on how secure their children feel, and, in turn, significantly affects their future emotional adjustment. Destructive forms of marital conflict—such as personal insults, defensiveness, marital withdrawal, sadness or fear—set in motion events that later led to emotional insecurity and maladjustment in children, including depression, anxiety and behavioral problems."* Pg. 159 Shoot the Damn Dog

Until reading about the results of this study, I

had never considered how my parent's failing marriage could have created an environment to foster depression. As I look at the lives of my siblings, each has battled substance abuse problems, in several instances leading to stints in rehab centers. More than one sibling finds solace in attending Alcoholics Anonymous meetings, sometimes several times a week. In no way do I blame my parents for whatever depressive effects their marriage had on me; they were fighting their own demons. For me, the most important take-away from the Cummings study is to hope the way I conducted myself in my own marriage when my children were in the house didn't create the conditions for them to be at-risk for depression.

Religion played almost no role in my early family life. However, my parents would occasionally load up the family station wagon and we'd depart for church services. On one such Sunday, I was walking to the family car when a fellow eight-year-old hurled a crab apple into the back of my head. A normal response might have been to retaliate by trying to hit him with my own crab apple. Or I might have simply told him that I didn't appreciate what he'd done and asked him to refrain from further assaults with these small projectiles. However, I did neither.

Within seconds of being hit, I had wrestled my nemesis to the sidewalk, and in front of a horrified departing congregation, commenced bashing his head into the concrete sidewalk in a fit of uncontrolled rage. A kindly neighbor who had built my parents' house reached down, grabbed me by the shoulders, and lifted me off my antagonist. Nothing more was said. That incident took place over fifty years ago, and it has bedeviled me since it occurred. Was my over-reaction to a childhood prank an indicator of dormant mental illness? Or had I been abused in some forgotten way that caused me to act out in such a violent manner? Or was I just having a bad day and snapped when a calmer response was warranted? I'll never know the answer, but I do know this: as a child, I took setbacks particularly hard. I'll never forget the shame and embarrassment I experienced as a twelve-year-old during a father-son golf tournament. It happened on the 12th hole when I hit a shot into the river. Tears flowed, and clubs were thrown.

      Throughout my battles with depression, I've wrestled with the nature v. nurture argument as to its origins. The case for a genetic cause seems irrefutable yet knowing of my mother's own struggles with the disease has caused me to consider how the development of my brain as an infant may have influenced me to retaliate as I did in the crab apple throwing incident, along with living out a life informed by the condition. I came across what for me was a startling revelation in a book about addiction. Dr. Gabor Maté is world renowned for his work in the field of substance abuse, having spent the better part of his career delivering palliative care to the most hard-core addicts in North America's only harm reduction treatment center in Vancouver, BC's Downtown Eastside. Harm reduction is a controversial approach in the field of addiction treatment, and, as I understand its workings, rests on the premise that a certain segment of society is going to engage in high risk behaviors, such as injecting heroin and other illicit drugs, and that rather than preaching platitudes such as Just Say No, a saner method of responding to addicts who have no hope of recovery is to reduce their suffering rather than seeking to treat them.

Maté's research points to the development of the infant brain as a precursor that shouldn't be overlooked. As he states in his compelling book *In the Realm of Hungry Ghosts*, *"Infants read, react to, and are developmentally influenced by the psychological states of the parents. In a very real sense, the parent's brain programs the infant's, and this is why stressed parents will often rear children whose stress apparatus also runs in high gear, no matter how much they love their child and no matter that they strive to do their best."*

Maté refers to a study conducted at the University of Washington in Seattle that compared the brains of two groups of six-month old infants. One group had mothers who suffered from postpartum depression, while the other group of mothers had normal moods. Measures of brain activity showed dramatic differences between the two groups. The babies of the depressed mothers had brain patterns characteristic of depression *"even during interactions with their mothers that were meant to elicit a joyful response."* Pg. 195 He also notes that levels of the stress hormone cortisol, which is associated with depression, were higher among the children of clinically depressed mothers. Maté concludes his chapter on brain development by observing, *"Since the brain governs mood . . ., we can expect that the neurological consequences of adverse experiences will lead to deficits in the personal and social lives of people who suffer them in childhood. Their predisposition to addiction was programmed in their early years. Their brains never had a chance."* Pg. 196 That last statement was made in relation to addiction and its origins but has caused me to wonder about its relevance to the genesis of depression. I *know* my mother cared for me and loved me in my infancy, but did limitations outside her control create the conditions for a depressed brain to develop?

The View from Under My Desk

Chapter 4: College Years and Early Self-Medicating

"Here is the tragedy: when you are the victim of depression, not only do you feel utterly helpless and abandoned by the world, you also know that very few people can understand, or even begin to believe, that life can be this painful." Giles Andreae

Amphetamines and Academia

Following high school graduation, I moved in for the summer with my family in Ketchum, the town adjacent to Sun Valley, and began teaching golf to the children of the wealthy summer residents at the Sun Valley Golf Club. I also began working in my father's store, Chateau Drug. The store would go on to become the gathering place for all sorts of folks, including a fair number of celebrities. The Ketchum/Sun Valley area has always been a haven for a variety of celebrities. Ernest Hemingway took his life in Ketchum, and my sister was pals with one of his granddaughters. In 2006, in no less a publication than the *New York Times*, a story would appear chronicling with amazement the vast array of goods my father had managed to squeeze into such a small retail space, with the reporter following around Tom Hanks, although not mentioning him by name, as he bantered with the help over which wrench to buy and what over-the-counter remedies the pharmacist recommended.

The store's friendly pharmacist during my college days had introduced me to the stimulant

Dexedrine to assist me in staying awake during my travels back and forth from college. I'd had an argument with my father over some long-forgotten issue while working at the store and was very upset. This took place during closing time at 9pm. My reaction to the conflict was to steal into the pharmacy, locate the Dexedrine, and take a handful of these drugs to self-medicate the pain from the battle with my father. My girlfriend was on hand and was horrified at my actions. I obviously didn't take enough to do any harm, other than to hyper stimulate my nervous system, but in hindsight, it's troubling to think I would behave in such a reckless manner.

Speaking of college and Sun Valley, I was surprised to learn that my first dormitory roommate was a fellow Sun Valley dweller. The probability of this was extremely low, given the resort's small population. He was a hard-core hippie (this was the '70's after all), who turned out to do some hardcore drugs. Not long after school began, my new roommate discovered the Sigma Alpha Epsilon fraternity, the number one-party frat on campus (think Animal House if you're old enough to remember that John Belushi movie). I never actually joined the fraternity but had many friends who did. As he was packing up to move into the frat house after a short stint as my roommate, he asked for a small favor: he was expecting a package in the mail, and would I be so kind as to bring it to him at his new abode?

After his mail arrived, I drove over to the SAE house and delivered the goods. He opened the book-shaped item, wrapped in brown butcher paper, and I watched in amazement as he tore it open. My short-term roommate had received a book, an innocuous enough mailing. However, as he ripped away the packaging, he opened the front cover to reveal that the pages had been hollowed out and its contents contained small, multicolored pieces of paper, each containing a powerful hit of LSD. An unfortunate footnote to this episode of hallucinogenic substances occurred when an SAE brother impregnated his girlfriend, who bore a child with severe birth defects, possibly attributable to his use of this psychedelic drug. The good brothers of Sigma Alpha Epsilon were true believers in mood-altering substances.

  It was in this milieu of drug use that these upperclassmen fraternity pals introduced me to a drug called Benzedrine, a stimulant that was used for pulling all-nighters prior to tests. I had no idea where my friends got them, but they were in abundant supply. Living with four wild seniors and grad students in a dive of a house, I adopted their approach to homework: neglect it throughout the semester, then study like mad the night before the test using chemically enhanced means.

  My introduction to bennies or crosstops, as they were called, seemed at first like I'd found nirvana until the horrific crash I experienced the day after the test. This turned out to be my first experience with self-medicating depression—I didn't know then that I was perhaps experiencing mild depression, just that the pills made me feel better. A photograph of the college golf team during my sophomore year clearly shows the face of a distraught young man. A night on these little white pills, combined with cigarettes, and coffee, alongside whatever textbook I studied from, was to experience a very pleasant high, all the while cramming every fact and figure necessary to pass the test, into my brain. When the tests were distributed, I was so wired I would write in every available space possible, including down the sides of the paper and on the back of the test leaving no white space. It was not uncommon during the next class period for the professor to announce that he wanted to read the most outstanding test. And guess whose test he read? The irony is that I recalled almost nothing of what I'd written.

But the crash the next day was worse than hell. My heart rate was off the charts, and my body was still so wound up that I once thought I was dying and the only thing I could think to do was call my girlfriend's mother and explain to her my dilemma (that I thought my death was imminent) and ask for her advice. She told me to go to the doctor, but I demurred, not wanting to disclose my use of illegal substances.

Benzedrine rewarded, and then it punished like mad. But these little pills offered a sure-fire way for me to ace any essay test during my sophomore year. However, the damage I was inflicting on my body was so intense, I made the difficult decision to forgo them my junior year. While I was high, and before the inevitable crash, I was having one of my first experiences in going from mild depression to euphoria, although short-lived. This experience with stimulants as an anti-depressant would resurface many years later with the dose of Adderall I'm now on. In light of my history with stimulants, I believe I could have easily become a meth addict.

Frozen with Despair on a Frozen Campus

"Many people experience the first symptoms of depression during their college years. Unfortunately, many college students who have depression aren't getting the help they need. They may not know where to go for help, or they may believe that treatment won't help. Others don't get help because they think their symptoms are just part of the typical stress of college, or they worry about being judged if they seek mental health care."
National Institute for Mental Health

I have a clear and distinct memory of being overcome with depression during my sophomore year. It was a bitterly cold winter day on campus, with snow covering the ground and frost on the trees. I had received two articles of clothing for Christmas in '71 on my trip to see the family for the holidays in Sun Valley: a black vinyl bomber jacket with a fleece collar, and some white Scott ski gloves, both of which I was wearing against the freezing temperature. I was standing on the northeast corner of the quad in the center of the campus, staring into the abyss. I was literally paralyzed. I couldn't will myself to go to my next class. All I could think about was dropping out of school. I had no idea what was happening to me, and no idea what to do to jolt myself out of my malaise.

Depression hadn't entered the popular lexicon as it has today, and I had no way of labeling what I was confronting. I just knew I was in pain but had no idea where it was coming from or what to do about it. I felt intolerable pain without a cause. I wanted relief, but it didn't even occur to me that what I was facing had a name, and that there were treatments available. So I stood there, frozen like the campus, with a feeling of overwhelming dread enveloping me. I didn't have a hangover, I hadn't broken up with my girlfriend (although that wasn't far off and would devastate me when it occurred), I wasn't physically ill, and I was injury free. Yet there I stood, fixated on the quad, and fixated on the fact that I was in unendurable agony for no identifiable reason.

My First Therapy Session—Less than Helpful

A short while later, I discovered the university offered counseling services, and I made an appointment to see a therapist, who turned out to be my advisor as well as a psychology professor, an aging hippie with a red goatee. My main memory of my one session with him was that, in an effort to put me at ease, he laid down on the floor with his back against the wall. Not much happened after I poured my heart out about my feelings of distress. Thus began my first experience with talk therapy, which has yet to make a dent in my mental illness, yet I hold out hope that I'll find a caring and competent therapist as my search continues.

The View from Under My Desk

      I believe it's worth noting that anxiety among college students has eclipsed depression as a condition this cohort seeks relief from by visits to campus counseling offices. *The New York Times* commented that, *"Anxiety has now surpassed depression as the most common mental health diagnosis among college students, though depression, too, is on the rise. More than half of students visiting campus clinics <u>cite anxiety as a health concern</u>, according to a recent study of more than 100,000 students nationwide by the Center for Collegiate Mental Health at Penn State. Nearly one in six college students <u>has been diagnosed with or treated for anxiety</u> within the last 12 months, according to the annual national survey by the American College Health Association.*

      The causes range widely, experts say, from mounting academic pressure at earlier ages to overprotective parents to compulsive engagement with social media. Anxiety has always played a role in the developmental drama of a student's life, but now more students experience anxiety so intense and overwhelming that they are seeking professional counseling." Anxious Students Strain College Mental Health Centers, May 27, 2015

Chapter 5: Transitions

"Depression is a disorder of mood, so mysteriously painful and elusive in the way it becomes known to the self—to the mediating intellect—as to verge close to being beyond description." William Styron, Darkness Visible

    Drugs and alcohol played a definite role during my college years. It's hard to know how much I used these substances to self-medicate. I do know that I was afraid of participating in class discussions. I was horribly self-conscious and feared making a fool of myself by raising my hand and making a comment or asking a question. But studying on Benzedrine made me feel like I was captain of the world, at least until its effects wore off. I regret not being a part of classroom discussions, especially when I had something to say, but censored myself out of fear of embarrassment. Perhaps these little white pills would have emboldened me to take part in class discussions. I'll never know. I don't believe I've completely conquered this reticence to speak up in a group, which is depressing and troubling. I hated grandstanders and must have felt like I'd rather recede into the background rather than expose my ignorance or be thought a know-it-all.
    I was an average student, although the drugs propelled me onto the dean's list one semester for getting straight A's, but that honor was tainted by the easiness of the courses I took, mostly in psychology. But put me in a class that demanded academic rigor,

like chemistry or computer science, and I was lost. I had no career aspirations, and only a vague idea of becoming an assistant golf pro at a course in Colorado, made likely by the golf coach and his connections there. Graduate school was never given a second thought, or maybe not even a first thought.

A Major Lifestyle Change

But love changed that. I started dating a girl whose father was a professor on campus, whose mother earned a master's degree after raising eight children, and who had siblings with high and noble academic aspirations, two of whom would earn PhD's and others would achieve master's degree status. A fellow student, an active Christian, decided I needed to date a young woman he knew, who also happened to share his faith. With much trepidation from the thought of going on a date with someone whose values were clearly different from my own, I agreed. To prepare for this encounter, I went to my mother's liquor cabinet and drank a few shots of vodka—not enough to get drunk, but just enough to quell the anxiety of the unknown.

Seeing the chaos of my own family's affairs, and being around Debbi's highly functional family, I became interested in making a life-style change and began adhering to her family's code of conduct. After things got serious, I approached her father about wedding his daughter and he wisely asked how I planned to support her. Seeing the blank look on my face, he picked up the phone, made a call to an old college buddy who had started an avant-garde master's program in organizational behavior at a major university, a two-hour drive from Logan, and the next thing I knew, I was being interviewed for a spot in the class of 1976. My only distinctive qualification, given a somewhat mediocre undergraduate stint, was that the school was looking for diversity, which meant anyone who hadn't gotten their undergraduate degree there. So I was in.

To pull off this feat financially, my new bride was called for a job interview by an elementary school in a low-income area of Salt Lake City on the day we were married. We found the only affordable housing in the area, a run-down attic on Salt Lake's busiest street, which hadn't been occupied for years. The place was a dive, and filthy to boot. Her kindly parents helped us move our meager household goods into our new love nest, and the four of us spent the afternoon and evening cleaning the grime away. My wife and I later learned that her mother was so distraught at the dreariness and decay of her beloved daughter's new living quarters that she drove back to Logan in tears. Thus began our lives as a couple.

As wonderful as it was to have my wife secure a teaching job at $7,000 per school year in one of the worst sections of town, it meant a one-hour commute for me to graduate school. Debbi would walk the three or so blocks to school each morning as I drove our sole car, that '70 Beetle, to my newly adopted campus. It was during this time that Ted Bundy, the notorious serial rapist and murderer, was on the loose in Salt Lake City. Debbi happened to look almost exactly like his victims, a slender build with long, brown hair. She also

The View from Under My Desk

happened to be the same age as those unfortunate young women Bundy brutalized. Seeing this, Debbi's fellow teachers had a stern talk with her: she would no longer walk to school—I would drop her off and pick her up. I dutifully obeyed.

Transitioning to a faith-based institution from Utah State University was an experience in culture shock. Not only had I gotten married a few days before classes started, a large enough life transition to handle by itself, but we were also living in a dump in the heart of a strange city. However, the worst was yet to come. Even though I was no longer a user of mood-altering substances, the culture of my new university couldn't have been more different from that of Utah State's. I'd gone from partying with the fraternity brothers to total immersion in a highly straight-laced culture, all within the span of a few weeks.

To be clear, I'd stopped drinking, drugging, and smoking prior to my senior year, but it was the cultural aspect of being around 25,000 fellow students who held strong beliefs about things I'd indulged in and enjoyed that I found disconcerting. I was a fish out of water in more ways than one. But the larger jolt came as I began classes amidst a group of fellow students, all of whom were older than myself, most with experience in full-time jobs and more than competitive in their efforts to one-up each other in classroom debates. The tension created by these classroom conflagrations precipitated a special session with two professors to attempt to manage these counterproductive encounters that were occurring with increasing frequency. Ashamed as I am to admit it, I was a retiring wallflower in these oftentimes acrimonious classes.

The Noonday Demon Doesn't Stop at Noon

And then depression kicked in. It happened every afternoon after I arrived home. I would attempt to study, only to get sidetracked into paralysis. I tried, I really did, but the energy and enthusiasm to hit the books wasn't there. It wasn't laziness; I was highly motivated to graduate with a degree that would enable me to begin a career. I would frequently start to study, only to end up with my head lying on the table, unable to will myself to persist. This was 1974, and depression medications, while available in cruder forms with more side effects did exist, I had no awareness of them. Nor did it occur to me that I was struggling with a mild mental illness. I was functional enough to eventually pull myself together, read the assignments, write the papers, and make class presentations, eventually completing an out-of-state internship, writing and defending my thesis, and earning a master's degree.

A few months prior to graduation, recruiters came calling. The hot, sexy company of the day for those in my field was Digital Equipment Corporation, or simply DEC. The company would later be purchased by Compaq, which was then bought by HP in a disastrous business decision. My best friend throughout graduate school was a larger than life fellow named Gary, a gregarious, ebullient good-looking bear of a man who landed a job with this Massachusetts based company. My first full-time job after graduation was as a training specialist with the Department of the Interior at Grand Coulee Dam, the nation's largest hydro-electric power plant, situated in the middle of nowhere in eastern Washington state. Our respective jobs couldn't have been more dissimilar—Gary's day-to-day life at DEC sounded exciting, faced-paced, and full of opportunities to ply his skills. His experience was a far cry from my often dull existence toiling away in the outback for one of Uncle Sam's agencies. I was more than envious.

I don't recall any issues with depression during my year and a half there: initially, it was an exciting time to actually be making a living wage, and my wife, along with our infant daughter and I, were embraced by the local workforce and seen as a breath of fresh air in a stodgy government facility. However, after taking a job in the lonely Washington desert with a less-than exciting government agency, I longed for the life Gary was living, as he'd recount the cutting-edge activities and industry heavy-hitters he'd rubbed shoulders with during our frequent coast-to-coast phone chats.

Longing to leave the moribund work life I was experiencing at The Bureau of Reclamation in my new hometown, Electric City (yes, that's actually a place on the map), I importuned Gary to lobby for me with his DEC superiors. Gary was kind enough to do so, securing three separate interviews, all of which I failed. I lacked his charm and charisma, his panache, his ability to instantly make you think you were life-long buddies. DEC's culture, which was fast and furious, would have chewed me up and spit me out. Getting a job there would have been disastrous. Somehow, I took the rejection in stride; perhaps I intuitively recognized the danger in venturing outside the low-key, safe and secure job I occupied in a federal agency. I was young, naive, and inexperienced, but had enough self-awareness that the best place for me at that stage of my career was right where I was.

      Depressives tend to take criticism especially hard. As a training specialist, owing to the small number of managers on site, I gave infrequent classes on management principles and communications skills. Each class ended with an evaluation from the participants. I conducted several classes during my time with the Bureau and can recall only one negative comment among the many positives. Someone had been annoyed at a phrase I had repeatedly used. I believe being so thin-skinned to such an innocuous comment was and is a symptom of depression. I expected every class to run perfectly smoothly—a completely unrealistic expectation—and this one slightly negative observation overrode all the positives. Defensiveness and an inability to readily accept criticism, whether constructive of not, isn't listed as a symptom of depression—at least I haven't seen it noted. However, as I look back on my career, the times I've received less than glowing appraisals have usually sent me spiraling. My inability to accept negative feedback when faced with a truly vicious personal attack would haunt me many years later, leading me to use narcotics to dull the pain of one particularly spiteful personal attack.

The View from Under My Desk

Chapter 6: My Career Takes Off—For the Most Part

"Work hard. And have patience. Because no matter who you are, you're going to get hurt in your career and you have to be patient to get through the injuries."
Randy Johnson

This quote is advice from the feared fastball artist of Major League Baseball fame and refers to the physical injuries professional athletes often sustain. My use of the quote is in the context of emotional injuries organizations inflict upon their members. As Mr. Johnson suggests, have patience, as I'll recount instances of incurring this type of damage in an office-based environment.

Boredom eventually settled in, and I was offered and accepted a job with a Fortune 50 forest products company in Eugene, Oregon. The local church congregation wholeheartedly embraced our little family of three, and we quickly had many friends. My biggest health struggle was physical, rather than mental. The area surrounding Eugene, which was deemed by *Money* magazine as the most desirable city in the country at the time, was the grass seed growing capital in the United States. The pollen generated by that particular industry caused me to have an extreme allergic reaction, to the point that I could barely breathe.

Fortunately, my body adapted, and with my progressive-minded boss, who was open to just about any idea I had for engaging this multi-plant organization in performance improvement efforts, I had free reign. As a still wet behind the ears 24-year old organizational consultant, I have to admit to floundering initially. But a random phone call changed me from a somewhat clueless neophyte trainer into a force that would impact this rough and unsophisticated group of lumber and plywood mills and the supervisors and managers who ran them.

A Career Breakthrough

The company, which was eventually purchased by International Paper, was, at least in those days, quite backward in its approach to management development and employee relations. I was seen by plant managers in the West Coast region as young, idealistic, naïve, inexperienced, and to some extent, a weird novelty with little if anything to contribute to their bottom lines. However, the phone call that would change everything occurred shortly after I began trying to figure out how I was going to infiltrate these factories in productive ways. A former fellow student was working for Exxon in a mine in Wyoming, and one day called me out of the blue to ask a long-forgotten question. We hadn't been particularly close in graduate school, although I liked and respected him, so the call came as something of a surprise. I asked what he was up to and he told me his company had engaged the services of a consulting firm out of Stamford, CT, ironically the locale of the headquarters office of my employer.

The View from Under My Desk

He described a new and exciting way of training managers in interpersonal skills, and I was instantly smitten, having just read a book about the very topic. After a long and hard-fought battle with my counterparts in the home office, spearheaded by my boss who believed in my vision for this major undertaking, the project got the green light and became all-consuming, and I was right in the center of it. I was even able to convince the crusty general manager over all the factories on the west coast to bring in a professor and team of doctoral students from Stanford to conduct research into the effects of the program. The results were highly positive, and I eventually co-authored an article in a refereed journal on our work in the mills with the Stanford professor—heady stuff for one not so academically inclined.

The Role of Gratitude

The nature of a depressed mind is to see the glass as half empty, ignoring, downplaying or taking for granted those aspects of life that are working, that give meaning and purpose, that the religious would refer to as blessings. The pain of a depressed mood makes reflecting upon the good things about life less likely. All that has or is going smoothly, along with thoughts of all the people who have come into one's life who've made a significant difference for good recede. I recently had an opportunity to battle this tendency when an unexpected Christmas card arrived at my house. It was from my former boss in the forest products company who had done so much to enable me to gain approval for the large-scale management training program I spearheaded, a responsibility handed to a 26-year-old kid with designs on transforming the culture of lumber and plywood mills run by rough hewn managers not predisposed to examining their interpersonal skills. Though I've often reflected on the improbability of someone so young and inexperienced being entrusted with overseeing, and eventually succeeding in creating large-scale organizational change, along with acknowledging in my mind my manager's essential role in paving the way for this effort I'd initiated, I've never thanked him for creating that opportunity, which I consider to be my most satisfying professional accomplishment. Now that I had Steve's new address in Oregon, I resolved to act, sending him my own Christmas card with a photo of my family, and writing on the back my appreciation for what'd he'd supported me in doing, and expressing the sentiment that he's the best boss I ever had. The comments I wrote were more than thirty years overdue, and it was time to share them. The feeling of satisfaction as I walked the card to the mailbox was palpable.

Psychology Today had this to say about the power of gratitude to lessen depressive symptoms: *"Why do these gratitude experiences boost happiness and alleviate depression? Scientists say that these techniques shift our thinking from negative outcomes to positive ones, elicit a surge of feel good <u>hormones</u> like <u>dopamine</u>,*
serotonin and <u>oxytocin</u>, and build enduring personal connections. The insight and reflection of counting

these moments is what makes the practice of gratitude so powerful. But the key to combating <u>depression</u> is making these positive experiences part of the fabric of your life."

Dr. Martin Seligman has formalized my simple thank you to my former boss in his "The Gratitude Visit" for which he provides precise instructions: *"Close your eyes. Call up the face of someone still alive who years ago did something or said something that changed your life for the better. Someone who you never properly thanked; someone you could meet face-to-face next week. Got a face?*

Gratitude can make your life happier and more satisfying. When we feel gratitude, we benefit from the pleasant memory of a positive event in our life. Also, when we express our gratitude to others, we strengthen our relationship with them. But sometimes our thank you is said so casually or quickly that it is nearly meaningless. In this exercise . . . you will have the opportunity to experience what it is like to express your gratitude in a thoughtful, purposeful manner.

Your task is to write a letter of gratitude to this individual and deliver it in person. The letter should be concrete and about three hundred words: be specific about what she did for you and how it affected your life. Let her know what you are doing now and mention how you often remember what she did. Make it sing! Once you have written the testimonial, call the person and tell her you'd like to visit her, but be vague about the purpose of the meeting; this exercise is much more fun when it is a surprise. When you meet her, take your time reading your letter."

The article describing Seligman's letter points out that, *"This somewhat self-consciousness-inducing exercise, Seligman promises, will make you happier and less depressed a mere month from now."*

https://www.brainpickings.org/2014/02/18/martin-seligman-gratitude-visit-three-blessings/

I decided to accept Seligman's challenge, and wrote the letter that follows. Since paying him a personal visit to read the letter wasn't possible, I called and read it over the phone. Here's what I said:

Dear Steve,

This letter is more than 30 years overdue. I mentioned on the back of the Christmas card I sent that you're the best boss I've ever had, and I've had quite a few. To say you were supportive to a wet behind the ears neophyte would be a serious understatement. Specifically, I came to you in 1978 with an audacious proposal, which was to hire the consulting firm in Stamford and that I would spearhead the initiative to implement what was then cutting-edge technology in training managers in interpersonal skills. As I look back on that experience, it's a minor miracle that it happened. There were so many things that could have prevented it from happening and the odds that the stodgy, hide bound company we worked for, with many old school naysayers in the home office to

The View from Under My Desk

squash that initiative, were long. Our company was probably one of the less enlightened large Fortune 500 companies to say the least, yet I naively and enthusiastically believed that program was the way to go. Had it not been for your support, the program would never have seen the light of day. Years later, I had great success in co-founding the Covey Leadership Center, and my efforts affected millions of lives. Yet I've occasionally reflected on what we did with the supervisory skills training program and consider it to be the highlight of my career. No twenty-six-year-old gets to propose and then implement a program that extensive in any large, bureaucratic organization, and I'm fully aware of how unique it was for me to have had that opportunity. And the credit for navigating the political waters to get it to happen is all yours. Your trust and belief in me were extraordinary, and though we've lost touch with one another, I'm forever grateful to you for your trust and your skill in creating this improbable opportunity for me.

    Your friend,
    Brad Anderson

Steve was touched, and he emotionally thanked me and asked for an emailed copy. Our friendship has now been rekindled and I got to experience the benefits of expressing gratitude.

I was, by now, skirting depression, at least most of the time. Some of my activities with this program took place in the early evenings at the company's largest factory, located in Lebanon, Oregon, a one-hour drive from my home in Eugene. I would often find myself in bed mid-afternoon prior to these events, a situation I now attribute to the depressive symptoms I was experiencing, even amidst the excitement and success I was having. At the time, I simply told myself I was tired and needed a rest prior to a long evening of training managers.

Anger

I believe anger has been a detriment to my happiness and success throughout my life, going all the way back to the episode on the church sidewalk as an eight-year-old hit with a crab apple. I also believe anger and becoming annoyed at small irritations is symptomatic of depression. For example, as 1980 was beginning and my project in the lumber and plywood mills was coming to an end, my boss, who had run interference for me throughout the politics of getting approval from the home office to implement this new program, quit the company and I was now on my own without a support system. The economy had gone south, and my boss saw little future in an industry that was about to get clobbered.

Having trained all the managers and supervisors in the lumber and plywood mills on the West Coast, I was at a loss for what to do next. I tried bringing in a consultant with a strong reputation in the forest products industry. I tried creating extensions of the program I'd been implementing. But nothing took. So, trying to be somewhat productive, I spent my days in a self-improvement

The View from Under My Desk

effort, holing up in the stacks in the University of Oregon library, reading journals in the behavioral sciences and trying to plot my next move with no organizational support, no budget, and little vision—a dreary existence after creating such a stir during the previous three years.

It was in this context that a couple of professors from the University of Oregon approached the general manager for whom I had done all this work, consulting with him without my involvement. In light of the three years I'd spent slogging it out in the trenches of his factories and garnering him accolades from the vice presidents in the home office, he'd failed to consult me, whose job it was to be involved in any and all organizational improvement efforts. From the general manager's point of view, he was just entertaining two local professors. I'm quite certain he had no malicious intent by not involving me, but being especially thin skinned, and lacking any meaningful work at the time, I interpreted his actions as villainous. This man's name was Al Smith. Al Smith was not a villain. However, I was acting like an immature rookie.

I took my non-involvement particularly hard, and upon learning of it, left the office for an angry round of golf to blow off steam. Absorbing setbacks in a calm and rational manner is not the province of the depressed. The renowned psychologist, Martin Seligman, has shown that depressed people internalize their misfortunes through ruminating about them, causing them to spiral ever downward into deeper and deeper depths. Seligman puts it this way, *"The more you are inclined to ruminate, the more it arises. The more it arises, the more depressed you will be. Brooding, thinking about how bad things are, starts the sequence."* Learned Optimism, Pg. 83 Another toxic effect of rumination is its effect on one's self-efficacy, which is a measure of the extent or strength of one's belief in one's own ability to complete tasks and reach goals. High and low self-efficacy determines whether someone will choose to take on a challenging task or "write it off" as impossible. I'm a ruminator and have found that challenging my pessimistic thoughts with more rational ones can short-circuit rumination when I remember to fight off this natural tendency.

I had experienced the general manager's failure to include me in discussions with the university professors as devastating: permanent (in spite of my resounding success with the supervisory training program, I was now a failure), pervasive (everything I tried in the future was doomed to be a losing cause) and personal (I had been excluded because of some noxious personality trait, or worse, because I was seen as incompetent). It took me a long time to recover and gather up the confidence I needed to move on. Depressed people are oftentimes not the most rational of creatures. Had I had the presence of mind to consider various scenarios that might have brought the professors into contact with Mr. Smith, I would have interpreted events much differently and behaved more maturely.

The View from Under My Desk

The Silicon Valley Beckons

It was now 1980, and the lumber industry was on the ropes, with interest rates at 20 percent and higher, driving housing starts to dramatic lows and killing the demand for lumber and plywood. Oregon wasn't in a recession—the economists declared it to be in a full-blown depression. Factories were laying off employees and demand for my services could only diminish, if not evaporate altogether. I desperately wanted to remain in the Northwest, but a depressed economy does not a favorable job market make.

That's when one of the most highly respected companies in America at the time came calling. Hewlett-Packard, known today as simply HP, was consistently rated as one of the best places to work in the nation. And two of their divisions wanted to interview me. Unfortunately, HP is today a shadow of its former self, but at the time was a highly sought-after place of employment. So I flew down to San Francisco and interviewed with both divisions, one in Palo Alto, the other in Santa Clara.

However, following two successful interviews, all was not smooth sailing. After receiving offers from both plants, Debbi and I couldn't make the money being offered square with our ability to survive financially in one of the most expensive housing markets in the U.S. So, I promptly rejected both offers and went back to my search in the Northwest. However, the Palo Alto division wasn't about to take no for an answer, and slightly increased their offer. By now, it was clear that jobs in Oregon weren't to be had, and we reluctantly accepted the higher offer in the heart of Silicon Valley. After three very happy years in Eugene, we were dreading the lifestyle that lay in store for us in the ultra congested, high cost of living environment of the Bay Area, separated from our friends, and I did not look forward to the prospect of a lengthy commute. Debbi spent many nights crying and I could do little to console her.

    I experienced one major setback at HP, and I reacted to it in much the same manner as I'd done in Oregon when the university professors approached "my" client, the general manager. HP had an unusual HR practice whereby each employee received a salary and performance review every three months and raises could be given during one of these reviews. My first two quarterly reviews had come out glowing, and at my nine-month review I fully, and naively, expected a pay raise.

    My family was barely scraping by financially, and I was growing desperate for more money in my paycheck. The only way we'd been able to buy a house was by using what was referred to as a wrap-around mortgage, a high-risk, draconian arrangement where the seller loaned the buyer the money for a very short period of time, after which the entire principle was due—referred to in the parlance of real estate agents as balloon payments. Ours was due after only three short years, but we hoped we'd be able to pay it as housing prices rose (as they'd done for years). Then we watched in horror as housing prices, once a seemingly guaranteed investment, stagnated and then began to drop. The prospect of losing everything seemed not only possible but likely.

Anger—Again

It was in this context that my next performance and salary reviews were held. After explaining that my performance over the past quarter had been excellent, my boss informed me that I would not be receiving a raise. When I heard the bad news, I reacted with extreme disappointment, frustration, and anger, storming out of his office in a fit of rage. In hindsight, my failure to control my temper was embarrassing and could have been cause for some type of discipline. The salary review took place near closing time, and I stalked out of my manager's office. I was livid and in total despair, emotions way out of proportion to events. Yes, I could have dearly used the extra money, but getting a pay bump after only nine months in the saddle, while possible, was far from a certainty. I lapsed into a state of despair, as rumination set in hard once again.

Perhaps I could have kept myself from spiraling had I practiced a simple idea developed by one of the founders of Cognitive Behavior Therapy, considered the gold standard in depression treatment, a man by the name of Albert Ellis. I had actually been exposed to this model in my first job with the government agency, when an outside consultant gave a seminar and handed out a little pamphlet summarizing its key points. It's been forty years ago, and I can still see the pamphlet in my mind. It was called *You Can Change the Way You Feel*. I should have read and re-read its message in the ensuing years.

Dr. Ellis came up with what he called the ABCDE model. Each letter in the sequence stands for one of the steps in the process, which can help someone think more rationally instead of letting emotions take over, as I did in the compensation discussion. Here's how it works. The A stands for Activating Event/Adversity, or the initial situation or "trigger." In my case, the activating event was being given the news that no raise in pay was planned. B stands for Belief System, or your interpretation of the situation, what you tell yourself about the event (your self talk) and your beliefs and expectations of others. My belief system was that I clearly deserved a raise at this review, obviously influenced by my personal financial situation, that my boss was expected to come through for me in light of my glowing performance over the past three months, and that he was being incredibly insensitive and callous by not raising my pay. C stands for Consequences, referring to how you feel and what you do in response to your belief system (the emotional and behavioral consequences). The consequences I experienced were anger, feelings of disrespect, ruminating on how awful I had it, and extreme disappointment. My self-talk was "How could he do this to me? This is awful! How can he not see the results I've produced and give me the raise I obviously deserved!" The D stands for Dispute, which refers to the process of examining your beliefs and expectations. Are they unrealistic or irrational?

The View from Under My Desk

If so, what may be an alternative, more rational appraisal of the situation? A more realistic interpretation is likely to lead to different, healthier emotional and behavioral consequences. Seligman adds an E to the sequence, which stands for Energization. This is a reflective step, which involves observing the increase in energy and vitality that occurs as you succeed in dealing with the negative beliefs. This final phase of the model creates a self-perpetuating reinforcement process that leads to the likelihood of using these steps when future adversities show up. I believe Solomon got it right when he stated that *"the opposite of depression isn't happiness; the opposite of depression is vitality."*

    I needed to dispute in a major way—which could have easily put an end to my unhealthy rumination. Using disputation could have included these arguments: there was no law on the books, or statement in the HP policy manual that an employee should receive a pay raise after nine months had elapsed. As an HR rep involved in coaching managers on compensation issues, I knew it was highly unusual for an employee to receive a raise in under a year's time. In fact, many employees didn't receive a raise for several quarters after a year had gone by. Disputing could have involved calling into question my assumption that a raise would be automatic, and that if one were granted, it would be highly unexpected. I could have also helped myself by recognizing that by purchasing the house, I had created my own financial hardship, and it was not the company's responsibility to bail me out of living on a highly restrictive budget. Sometimes, little pamphlets passed out in seminars can save a ton of distress.

The View from Under My Desk

Chapter 7: Success and Setback in a Startup

"With power comes the abuse of power. It's nothing new." Judd Rose

After a few months at HP, where I was required to perform a variety of HR duties I detested, I could see there was no career path for me to follow. Anyone inhabiting a role in an HR department was expected to learn all its functions and hope to one day be promoted to HR manager, an aspiration I didn't hold. My great love was management training. An old friend from graduate school had left his PhD program at Stanford and took a teaching position at a major university in Utah, but his passion lay in creating a startup that would improve on the lessons he'd learned in school while researching the program I'd implemented at the lumber company. So after a little over two years with HP, I packed up my family and moved back to Utah to begin work with a startup, a group with hardly any working capital, but with the promise of big things to come. I was making the leap from a highly stable company to begin work with a tiny training company that hardly anyone had heard of. Debbi was thrilled, as the move would put her in much closer proximity to her family, so it was off to the Beehive State to seek my fortune amidst the shakiest of financial circumstances.

The new company had five employees, counting myself, and no one knew anything about marketing, pitting us against well-established training companies that possessed inferior programs but with much wider market recognition. Thanks to my Stanford friend's creativity, the company had a superior product, but lacked the ability to spread the word. Money was tight. One day, the CEO called a meeting and asked this troubling question: "Whose house payment is due the soonest?" That was his way of letting everyone know the dire financial straits the company was in. But in spite of ourselves, word got out about our new program, and there was always just enough money to make payroll.

At just about the time the company was going to fold, a Fortune 500 company in Chicago found out about us and I took the call. They'd done their due diligence, looked us up on Dun and Bradstreet, liked our program, and knew we were on the ropes. This led them to make an offer that under better circumstances we would have scoffed at, but I became a temporary hero by engineering a deal whereby this client would purchase outright the ability to use our program with no additional participant or licensing fees, which was the typical pricing model in the industry. They got our program at a fire sale price, after I lobbied my colleagues that we had to take their cutthroat offer, granting them unlimited rights to a program that should have cost in the hundreds of thousands of dollars. But my finagling brought in a desperately needed infusion of cash and allowed the doors to stay open until new clients could be acquired.

The company had one investor, an elderly gentleman from Southern California, who'd anted up some money to get things off the ground. Unfortunately, he'd suffered a stroke, and his mental capacities had declined dramatically. Yet, in spite of

The View from Under My Desk

diminished cognitive abilities, he insisted on a role in running the company. This created a nightmare scenario for the CEO, who resigned in disgust, leaving the company rudderless and in dire straits.

Tom, the elderly investor, took it upon himself to conduct an executive search by running an expensive ad in a national business publication. Without consulting those of us who would have to work with a new CEO, he ended up hiring a sales manager from a Fortune 50 company who seemed to have one goal in mind: ratchet up the value of the company and sell it. This created a serious culture clash with the rest of us, who were on a mission to change the world through improving managerial effectiveness. We were all making modest salaries and, while each of us would have definitely enjoyed a raise in pay, we weren't in it for the money. We believed that would come in time if we could achieve the success that appeared to lie ahead.

Excitement Turns to Despair

The new leader ended up creating a stock ownership plan, and guess who got the lion's share of ownership? This helps to explain one of the most challenging incidents I've had the misfortune of experiencing in my 40-year career. Somehow the great American car manufacturer, General Motors, came calling. This was like manna from heaven for a small, struggling startup. Frank, the new CEO and I flew to Detroit to make our pitch. I would do the formal presentation, showcasing the program's features and benefits, and he would close the deal.

Miraculously, it worked—the car-making giant wanted to implement our program! Happier days could not be imagined. But the euphoria was not to last once we arrived back in Utah and informed the rest of the staff of our success.

    Ed, one of my counterparts who, like me, conducted client trainings, had been assigned prior to our trip to be the GM account manager, no small win for him as potential commissions could be huge with this legend of a company. But the new CEO had different ideas for divvying up the yet-to-be earned wealth now that the deal was closed. He informed Ed, in my presence, that GM was going to be a "house account" meaning that no one would receive commissions, this in spite of his earlier promise to Ed regarding his potential windfall from a giant company that wanted a lot of training from our meager little firm. I had yet to be exposed to Frank's management practices, but that would soon change.

    After the CEO declared his intention to make GM a house account, Ed put up a mild defense of himself, as this meant he was about to take a huge financial hit, but it was to no avail. With nothing to gain other than my self-respect, I spoke up in defense of Ed. I explained how I'd been present when Frank had assigned GM to Ed, and that it was his account, and that commissions generated from GM should flow directly to Ed. Instead of addressing the issue of commissions, much to my surprise, Frank turned his attention to me.

    How dare I be so disrespectful as to counter his point? Who did I think I was to go against his edict? What gave me the right to clarify a

The View from Under My Desk

misunderstanding? In other words, who the hell did I think I was to stand up to him? It appeared to me, at least, that his intention was to retain all the GM revenues within the company's coffers so that he could skim off whatever amount he wanted.

It was now well past 6 pm, and after two hours of being berated for my audacious arrogance in Ed's defense, I explained that my kindergarten-aged son had a class performance at the elementary school, and that I needed to leave. Rather than terminate his verbal onslaught since he'd clearly made his point that he was never to be challenged, Frank announced we would all reconvene after the five year olds had performed, to continue his verbal harangue against me. And that's what we did. I despondently met my wife and child at the school but was unable to enjoy the children's performance in light of having been thoroughly raked over the coals, with more to come following the show.

So, promptly at the appointed hour, which was 8pm, I settled in to hear more comments about my impertinent behavior. This would go on for another two hours. As I drove home, completely destroyed by my attempt to defend Ed's commissions, I wondered how I could survive in this environment. Welcome to entrepreneurship.

The ambush toward me seemed to validate Seligman's assertions about pessimists, who are much more likely to be depressed. According to Frank, I was personally defective, my failings pervaded my entire being, and I was permanently a loser—personal, pervasive, and permanent flaws that had just been meted out over a four-hour torture session.

Channeling Adversity into a New Opportunity

But life would soon change as Ed was about to jump ship, a decision that would have enormous implications for me. He'd been a graduate assistant to Dr. Stephen R. Covey, an adjunct professor and prolific speaker to several major organizations and had stayed close to him after graduation. Upon learning that Stephen was leaving the university to start a consulting business, Ed wisely left Frank and the rest of us for greener pastures. His role was to help promote Covey's speaking engagements. After enduring a few more months of Frank's management style, I decided to act. It was Halloween night, 1984. I was sitting in my Romulus, Michigan, Hilton Hotel room, hard by the Detroit airport, conducting a two-day training session for GM, and decided it was time to get out.

In light of what appeared to be a bleak future, I desperately needed to find new employment, so I picked up the phone and dialed Ed. Could he arrange a meeting with Stephen's CEO? A time was set, during which the CEO, a visionary businessman named Bill, handed me a three-cassette audio lecture Covey had delivered in a local high school auditorium for me to become more acquainted with the company's content. This was the only documented material of the *Seven Habits of Highly Effective People*—amazingly, nothing had been written down, and I eagerly accepted listening to this

The View from Under My Desk

presentation, hoping to learn more about this new theory of personal and interpersonal excellence.

Chapter 8: Seven Habits of Highly Effective People

"Great life lessons taught by a great man. He not only taught lessons he also lived the lessons." from a review on Amazon.com

The more I listened to those tapes, the more I became convinced that Stephen had tapped into the zeitgeist–the spirit of the times. Maybe Covey was on to something—that character counted. I began to ask myself the question of whether Stephen's *Seven Habits* had the potential to be of value to leaders, managers, and employees alike. After having spent so many years teaching skills, it occurred to me that the mood in Corporate America was shifting–that organization's were hungering for a different message; in Covey's case, he was promoting a much different philosophy than the one I'd built my career on—that the way one lives his or her own life, their character, mattered as much, if not more, than techniques and skills. And then it hit me—Covey needed someone to create the means of communicating his teachings to the world.

Stephen taught that before you could become effective at the interpersonal level, you first had to acquire self-mastery, which meant keeping your emotions in check and developing self-control. He called it achieving a private victory, and his mantra was that private victories over self had to precede public victories where others were involved. I reflected upon all the one-on-one tutorials I'd had with hot-headed supervisors, many of whom had gone through my skills-based training courses, and how they continually failed at controlling their tempers, never mastering the private victory, regardless of how many times we went over the interpersonal skills required of their jobs.

Covey's approach didn't dismiss skill training but rested on the assumption that skill training alone was insufficient to properly equip managers for the daily battles they fought out in the trenches. The more I listened to the tapes, the more convinced I became that Stephen had a compelling message and started to see how I might have a role in bringing the *Seven Habits* to the masses.

It all made sense. I became a believer, intent on spreading the message that one progresses from a state of dependence, to independence, and finally to interdependence. You couldn't work effectively at the interdependent, or collaborative level, unless you first had your personal act together. I'd witnessed it firsthand, and now here was someone who'd codified it into a system, but needed help getting it to the world. That's where I would make my play to become a part of this new approach to becoming "highly effective." I would create a packaged program for corporate America, a package that solved the riddle of why straight-on interpersonal skills training failed so often to achieve its goals.

A Career Breakthrough

It was in this context in early 1985 that I made my appeal to Stephen and his CEO to allow me to develop a way of packaging his message, and to my delight, they both agreed. In hindsight, my proposal lacked one crucial but overlooked component: marketing, a fact that would make selling my program in the early days quite problematic to a world unfamiliar with Dr. Covey's habits, very unlike today, where "win-win" (Habit 4) is ubiquitous. I'd assumed that if you built it, they would come. But once his book hit the shelves in 1989, the world beat a path to our doorstep. Salespeople were no longer having to try to explain the pronunciation of Covey's name ("no, it's Covey, like a covey of quail, not CO-vay"). Due to the popularity of the book, making a sale of the three-day seminar I'd developed became more of an exercise in order taking than selling.

Once I started working at the Covey Leadership Center (now Franklin-Covey), I quickly realized that being assigned a desk in a bullpen like area among the other five or six employees wasn't going to work. The job demanded complete concentration, and the normal routines in any office of answering phones, conversations between employees, and various other distractions did anything but afford an atmosphere of silence. So, I went exploring, and found a large, unfinished room nearby, with wall studs exposed, electrical conduit strung this way and that and a plywood floor. And best of all, there were no phones, and no one knew

The View from Under My Desk

about my new hangout.

It was within this milieu that I began a series of interviews with Stephen to begin to extract from him the kernels of wisdom that I was certain just needed to be mined. And to my delight, he began describing the Seven Habits in a depth that had never been explored. He began an extensive description of the principles that undergirded his speeches, which were always time bound, never allowing him to dive deeply into these ideas. And to his credit, he never once commented on our surroundings, which in addition to the unfinished room, consisted of office décor that featured two small end tables that served as our desks, and a couple of pirated chairs. I'm certain this was not his typical work setting.

I must have become somewhat of an annoyance to him, as I secreted him off to our unknown locale whenever I saw him in the office. He was always more than enthusiastic to resume our endeavor, which was designed to produce the outline of a six-day video shoot a few months off. I took every opportunity to corral him into yet another interview. It was during this phase of the project that I began my strategy of driving him to the airport in my car that did, in fact, come fully equipped with a heater.

Finally, after months of planning, the big day arrived for the first video shoot. It was to take place before a studio audience to take it out of the realm of a talking head, as well as to enable Stephen to what he is so brilliant at–interacting with his audience. That first day got off to a less than superb start. Stephen seemed unsure of himself in this new, staged environment, was going off script, and to worsen matters, there was one technical problem after another. At one point, the power for that entire area of Salt Lake went out. Cameras went dead. Audio equipment stopped functioning. The audience began to stir. I recall frantically running out into the middle of the room, assuring the audience that things would be back to normal in no time (a complete fabrication, but what else could I do?). I then used that enforced down time to huddle with Stephen to help him focus on our outline. Once power was restored, he became a new man, presenting his material with passion, eloquence, all the while using our outline to guide his delivery.

Following the shoot, the tedious and time-consuming task of viewing every second of dozens of hours of video tape began. The goal was to identify those segments from his presentation that packed the most punch, all done with an eye on the next phase, which was performing the final edit under the direction of a professional video editor at a studio, with a fee of $400/hr. I would later learn that the editing costs I incurred had nearly bankrupted the company. Early on in this extremely expensive process (digital media has since lowered the cost of editing so that any high school student with a cell phone and a laptop can produce decent quality video), the editor pointed out what would become a major impediment to creating a finished product. For a few nail-biting weeks, this looked to have the potential to completely derail the editing process, destroying those arduous days of filming Stephen. Briefly, it involved a term editor call print through.

The View from Under My Desk

Print through, which no longer occurs with the advent of digital video, occurs when electrical particles from one portion of the tape are transmitted to the next layer of tape in the wound cassette containing a roll of 2-inch videotape. The result was that the audio from the adjoining layer of tape could be faintly, but distinctly heard on the portion of tape showing Stephen speaking on the segment we wanted to hear. This created an entirely unacceptable video. After a great deal of hand wringing and the accompanying angst I was experiencing, a highly skilled senior editor eventually resolved the problem.

    As I look back on experiences such as this one, along with the constant setbacks along the way to creating a successful program, I'm struck by my resilience in the face of all the adversities, resilience that has since diminished somewhat. Perhaps the most devastating event to occur as the project neared completion was when I received an unexpected call from the manager of training at one of Stephen's speaking clients. An important component of my pitch to Stephen and his CEO to develop the program was that I would raise the money for the production through corporate sponsorships. So I had in essence, signed up to accomplish two major goals: fund raising and development of the program. In preparing to hit the road to ask several of Stephen's speaking clients to help underwrite the production costs, I hired a courtroom artist to create visuals of some of the still images I had in mind to enhance Stephen's speech. I carried these in a large briefcase and used them to create a visual picture for the executives I was about to encounter, with the hope that seeing was better than listening to me extoll the value of coming onboard as an investor. The offer was for a sponsoring company to invest anywhere from $5,000 to $20,000 upfront, and in return, they would be given unlimited rights to train as many people as they wanted–an incredible offer, but only if I could deliver. Compared to the pricing model we would employ after finalizing and launching the program, this represented a steal of major proportions. Comparing the amount spent on a sponsorship to our projected pricing, this was the essential part of my presentation to these early sponsors–to get in on the ground floor for a somewhat small investment, and in return, receive an enormous discount for having rolled the dice.

Encountering a Major Setback

The manager who called introduced herself as head of training for one of the large sponsors I'd met with–all senior executives, including the CEO, who had happily agreed to participate. She had learned of her organization's decision to participate as a sponsor, and said she'd like me to come to her organization to deliver a pilot program. This was a completely reasonable request, and a date was set.

During our initial encounter on the morning of the first of five days of pilot training, I knew something was off, but couldn't quite identify what was troubling me. The plan she'd proposed was that I would conduct the training from 8:00 am to noon, after which she and her colleague would meet with me to provide feedback on their observations. The

The View from Under My Desk

two of them sat in the back of the room, and at one point, I noticed them furiously scribbling out notes, my first indication that all was not what I had been led to believe. The afternoon feedback sessions for the first four days were somewhat cordial, and the feedback useful–no red flags I could foresee. But on Friday, all hell broke loose. In a major departure from the tone of the other four meetings, she and her partner attacked with a vengenence. My gut instinct on the first morning was proving to be valid. For four straight hours, I was accused of covertly delivering a message, masquerading as leadership training, of a philosophy and pattern of living they saw as not only wrong, but unethical. My only defense during this onslaught, was to keep pointing to the participant evaluations from the twenty or so managers who had attended, which were 100% positive, containing comment after comment referring to the training as "life changing," along with checking off boxes with 10's on a 10 point scale next to questions such as "I would highly recommend that others attend this training" and "This training has given me practical skills to be a better manager."

  As I vainly attempted to understand the reasons for their accusations, asking for specific examples of what lay behind their concerns, I made zero progress. After four gut-wrenching hours of invective, 5:00 pm mercifully arrived. My misery was over, or so I thought. The stated goal of conducting the training to receive important feedback had been revealed for what it was–a means of retaliation for not involving her in the decision to bring this program into her organization.

Having been in her exact role in several organizations, my failure to include her in the meeting with the executives was no rookie mistake. Earlier, I described my angry reaction when I learned that I had been left out of the lumber company's executive's discussions with a team of outside consultants. My naiveté in not including this major stakeholder, whose job was to serve as gate keeper for all training conducted in her organization, had set in motion a severe setback to the progress I'd been making.

I returned home with what should have been optimism and confidence in what I'd delivered. But the painful experience of that Friday afternoon prevented any such emotions to be felt. I had been blindsided and had only myself to blame. However, as difficult as that experience was, the worst was yet to come. My "host" had contacted the company's executive vice president, who was involved in my sponsorship presentation and had been an enthusiastic supporter and reported her conclusions. This EVP immediately called Stephen, outraged over the damaging claims he'd just heard. He demanded a full refund of their sponsorship contribution, and told Stephen and Bill, the CEO, to never contact them again. Not only had I alienated one of Stephen's long-standing clients, to say nothing of the disappearance of the valuable sponsorship fee, Stephen had been embarrassed, and had lost a relationship he'd valued for years. This episode caused me to lose valuable time I should have been devoting to the project, as I attempted to do damage

The View from Under My Desk

control all around.

 In spite of setbacks like the videotape problem and losing a valued sponsor, I pushed ahead–behaviors that would be significantly more difficult to do today. Years later, unable to find any kind of work in my field, I took an $8/hour job in a small ski shop. Business was often slow, and one day I found myself goggling "Is depression a progressive disease?" on my phone. I don't recall the search results, but there's no question in my mind that the answer, at least in my case, is "yes." I look back on that period of frenetic and successful activity with a mix of pride and despair. Pride because of the accomplishment, aided by too many people to mention, and despair at the realization that I can't see myself entering, much less completing a project of that scope. One characteristic of the depressive mind is that setbacks such as the many I encountered throughout the eighteen-month development process, often lead to states of mind antithetical to productive work. Pessimism and self-doubt begin to crowd out prior optimistic thoughts, often leading the individual to throw in the towel and give up. How then, was I able to see this and many other projects to completion? My best response is embodied in the question I typed into my phone 30 years later. As I've tried to illustrate in earlier chapters, I did, in fact, demonstrate hints of depression in my earlier years. But they were mild enough, and infrequent enough, that they didn't create any major impediments to successfully fulfilling my job responsibilities in those bygone days.

 So how then, in the many years of worsening

depression since those halcyon days of tireless and fulfilling work, with the devastation depression has imposed on my life, and with no treatment options available as I've tried just about all the remedies psychiatry and therapy have at their disposal, am I able to not succumb to the obvious way out (at least to me it's obvious), and just end it all? There are two primary reasons: the life-altering consequences this would impose on my family, and the hope that I will one day be restored to normalcy, or at least, experience less of the burdens this condition imposes. I believe a legitimate question to ask, considering all the effort and money and hope I've invested in seeking relief, would be: what basis for hope could you possibly have? For anyone experiencing depression, for anyone who cares about someone suffering from depression and for anyone who wants to become educated about the disease, Styron's book, *Darkness Visible*, first published in 1990, stands as a beacon of hope, not just for me, but for millions of sufferers. Styron's account of his own descent into the abyss, and his eventual recovery, was the first time the public had access to a brilliantly written description of the horrors of the disease, and the knowledge that someone who had been into the darkest of places, including suicidality, recovered and regained his mental health. The book was a major breakthrough in diminishing the stigma of mental illness and became required reading in many medical schools. I recently came across a podcast called *The Great God of Depression*, available on Showcase from PRX's Radiotopia. This five-episode series includes interviews with Styron and provides insights into his battles that had not been available.

This quote from *Darkness Visible* in one example of how I'm able to retain hope:

"For those who have dwelt in depression's dark wood, and known its inexplicable agony, their return from the abyss is not unlike the ascent of the poet, trudging upward and upward out of hell's black depths and at last emerging into what he saw as "the shining world." There, whoever has been restored to health has almost always been restored to the capacity for serenity and joy, and this may be indemnity enough for having endured the despair beyond despair.

Returning to completing *The Seven Habits* program, the trainer guide was finished, along with the accompanying participant workbook. After encountering the realities facing anyone undertaking the creation of something new and norm-breaking, we were finally ready to launch this brand-new creation to the corporate world. With great anticipation, and with the help of several talented and committed members of this now growing organization, our first group of real clients were assembled at Robert Redford's Sundance Resort to experience a new type of leadership training. The week went better than I'd expected, and I recall driving home on that Friday afternoon and literally collapsing onto my bed from sheer but satisfying exhaustion. We'd done it! Now let's go tell the world! The gamble taken by Stephen and Bill, the CEO, to give me the green light had paid off handsomely. The program became the cash cow of the company, which was immensely enabled when Stephen's bestseller was published in 1989. Almost thirty years later, the book is still popular. The last figure I saw was twenty-five million copies in print.

From my early days at the Covey organization in the spring of '85 until I eventually left the company, and in spite of intermittent bouts with depression, one of which I described in Chapter 2, when I became practically immobilized with despair, my team and I were busily, and often happily engaged in churning out ever more products to help clients become more highly effective. This is not to suggest that I was the perfect executive, in fact, far from it. And this organization, like any other, had its share of disruptions and conflicts that arise anytime a group comes together to work towards their goals, which are hopefully aligned with the company's mission and values.

Caught Off Guard

It was now 1996, and the company's success had been meteoric. Revenues were flowing in from many parts of the world. Stephen had been featured on the front page of *USA Today's* Money section, had been the focus of a major story in *Fortune Magazine*, and *Business Week* had come calling. He was at the height of his fame, and the company's revenues were making dramatic gains year over year.

The View from Under My Desk

The program I'd developed was being delivered to tens of thousands, now in the millions. Yet, for all this seeming success, net profits were dismal. Yet with all this worldwide attention contributing to ever rising revenues, costs were out of control, and the board became alarmed.

It was in this context that I experienced a significant depressive episode, but unlike the one described in the all-day executive meeting, where there were no precipitating events to induce depression, this one was different. I was invited to attend a meeting called by a fellow executive I'll call Charlie. Charlie, like myself, had joined the company in its beginning days. We had worked closely together on numerous occasions, as his department provided valuable services to me and the other members of the product development team. Over the years, we had become close, often going to lunch together, sharing our triumphs as well as failures with one another. I had grown to trust Charlie and saw him as an essential ally in our efforts to accomplish the company's mission. I viewed him as more than just competent leader, considering him a friend, an individual I respected and admired for his commitment to the company's goals. We had spent many hours through the years discussing how each of us could improve our respective functions, and I'd benefitted more times than I can recall from his wise advice. I had always thought that he had my back, and that I had his.

The stated agenda of the meeting was to discuss ways of streamlining certain functions in Charlie's department in an effort to increase quality and reduce costs. I arrived and noticed that Charlie and Jackie, one of his key lieutenants who had joined the organization fresh out of an Ivy League university, with impeccable credentials, were huddled in the far corner of the room. Everyone saw her as a rising star, as she had demonstrated exceptional judgment, particularly for someone new to the work force. I was the only other person present. The two of them seemed to be in a confidential conversation, given their body language and hushed tones they were speaking in. I retreated to the reception area to give them their space and waited for the others to arrive.

    Soon, the other attendees showed up, about ten of us in total, and we sat in a circle. Charlie got quickly to the point. The purpose of the meeting, we were told, was to consider a new, untried system and that Charlie had assigned Jackie to research this approach. Before going ahead with its implementation, Charlie wanted to know what the others of us, all stakeholders in his area of responsibility, thought of this proposal. Jackie then described her findings and the recommendation she had made to Charlie to put this system to work as soon as possible. As I listened to her report, I began to have some misgivings, based upon my prior experience with a similar system at a previous employer. I knew that there would be an appropriate time to share my concerns and waited for her presentation to end. Charlie then began the process of engaging the group in a discussion, which gave me the impression that the decision to go ahead with Jackie's proposal rested upon our ability to achieve consensus. Further, he informed us that, since each person in attendance represented an area of the company that would be affected by whatever system was adopted, our opinions mattered. And with that, the polling began.

As the discussion progressed, I was surprised at how quickly everyone expressed their support for Jackie's pitch–everyone with the exception of another long-time player by the name of Mel, as well as myself. As I finished sharing my concerns from past experiences with an almost exact replica of this new plan that would have a major impact on us all, I received a shocking and completely unexpected reaction. I was seated directly to Charlie's right, and he turned to me, face on, and made this statement with an expression and tone that exuded pure disgust. His exact words were: "Jackie gets it! You don't get it!" I was beyond stunned. Psychologists have a way of describing someone's reaction in situations that provoke feelings of fear, danger, attack and uncertainty, feelings I was now distressed by from Charlie's startling attack upon my feedback. Unless we are aware of and have been trained in other, more effective ways of dealing with these conditions, which doesn't always guarantee a successful outcome, but does increase the likelihood of achieving better results, most tend toward one of three modes of coping with unexpected and problematic interpersonal situations: they resort to either flight (get me out of here as soon as possible); fight (self explanatory: push back hard, and try to overpower your adversary); or freeze (the body's response when someone or something may be threatening to cause you physical or psychological harm). Freezing often occurs with victims of sexual abuse and violence. I had gone into freeze mode.

As I indicated above, for over ten years, I'd spent countless hours in one-on-one meetings with Charlie, mapping out strategies to enable the company to adapt to the fast pace of growth. I was among his most loyal cohorts. And until that moment, he'd treated me with nothing but respect and gratitude for my contributions. I'd never had a harsh word with the man. And now I was hearing, in the sternest of tones, that my opinion was not only worthless, but that I was devoid of the ability to understand the proposal.

No one's perfect—I get that as well as anyone. I had just made a comment indicating a serious concern with Jackie's proposal. And rather than exploring the arguments that Mel and I had voiced, he'd turned on me in an angry and confrontational manner. In a less fraught environment, I could have behaved differently as well. I wish I could have a do-over with this interchange. I could have inquired as to what lay behind his out of character and highly emotional response, asking why he considered my comments to be invalid. I could have challenged his dismissive tone. These would have been appropriate responses, ones requiring presence of mind, along with a bit of humility. Rather than freezing, I could have attempted another way of dealing with him, an approach some refer to as dialogue. But I was so caught off guard I simply sat there, too taken aback to even reply. I blame myself for allowing my comments about the proposal to be dismissed out of hand, and for not confronting Charlie's comment with maturity and inquisitiveness. I blame myself for freezing.

    As the meeting progressed (or devolved, depending on your interpretation) it was becoming clear that the decision to move forward with Jackie's recommendation was a fait accompli— something that has already happened or been decided before those affected hear about it, leaving them with no option but to accept it. By now, it seemed clear to me that this decision had been made prior to the meeting, and we were there to rubber stamp it. Charlie created the impression of seeking consensus, but this was not what he'd wanted from the group. Charlie was determined to forge ahead with what he and Jackie wanted. With the benefit of hindsight, Charlie's decision to implement Jackie's proposal as quickly as possible makes perfect sense. He was under tremendous pressure from the board to resolve the problems that had plagued his department for some time and saw Jackie's plan as his way to both address the issues hindering his department's performance and reputation, and to ease the anxiety created by being in the board's headlights.

    To his credit, Charlie had learned about my concerns with his confrontational method of addressing me and sought me out at a company party to apologize. I willingly accepted this overture and mentioned my embarrassment of not approaching him after tempers had subsided to restore the relationship and to no assure him that I wouldn't allow the incident to interfere with our future dealings. Had I initiated a conversation to debrief the meeting, I could have pointed out two issues beyond his approach with me. Being called to a meeting for achieving consensus, and to then learn the true reason for gathering us, I would have informed him of two consequences that ensued, both of which I was certain he hadn't intended. One was that, by misrepresenting the meeting's purpose, I had come away feeling manipulated. And secondly, his words combined with his tone, delivered in a setting of my peers, created embarrassment and shame.

    Depressive people tend to be thin-skinned when criticized and can become devastated at even a minor suggestion of how they could improve future performance. In an upcoming chapter, I'll describe the dread I felt prior to every weekly meeting my boss had scheduled to review my past week's performance, knowing with a high degree of certainty the censure, bordering on contempt, which I would endure, along with the complete absence of any form of validation. Charlie's shocking manner of addressing me, exacerbated by being called out in front of a group, was more damaging than a simple piece of feedback. I could have greatly reduced the emotional pain I experienced had I acted prior to Charlie's apology.

Seven Habits 2.0

    As the initial version of the Seven Habits program was maturing, I recognized the need to update and make improvements I'd had on my mind for some time. The plan was to produce short films to illustrate each of the Seven Habits. I saw this a way to both validate the principles embodied in the habits, as well to enhance the entertainment value of the training. The result was the production of over a dozen short films, almost all of which won top awards in various film festivals. They were either documentaries or short dramatic pieces, lasting from five to twenty minutes. The films were an untested and risky departure from other training programs, and clients ate them up. Stephen used several of these pieces in his speeches, and one was picked up by the local PBS station in Chicago and aired to critical acclaim. To be clear, I'm not now, nor have I ever been, a filmmaker. I came up with the idea to enhance what was an already a much sought-after training program and was fortunate to connect with a talented filmmaker, who shared my vision and enthusiasm for venturing into territory other firms in the industry weren't doing. Without his experience, wisdom and expertise, the films could have flopped. The competitive advantage these films created is hard to measure, but client after client talked about how much they enhanced the program and were often amazed at the production values in these short pieces.

  During one of our extended filming trips to Africa, which included a visit to the island of Mauritius in the Indian Ocean, I was dreading being on this lengthy trip and becoming depressed. A short time before our crew departed on this three-week journey, I paid a visit to a hand surgeon who'd operated on my finger to remove an annoying calcium deposit. Having on occasion experienced some temporary relief from depression from prescription painkillers, I told this doctor that I had back pain and asked for a prescription of Lortab, an opiate with potential addictive results. I'm not proud about lying to the doctor but saw no other remedy. He complied, and I felt I had a solution to any depression that might beset me on the trip. I recall becoming terrified upon going through customs in Mauritius. As you entered the customs area, you couldn't help but notice a huge sign proclaiming that anyone found with illegal drugs would be executed. Even though I was in possession of a legitimate prescription for the painkillers in my luggage, I envisioned myself being sent off to the execution chambers of this tiny island. Ironically, when I did begin to experience a depressed mood, I popped a pill into my mouth and immediately became severely nauseated. Instead of relief, I was in a state of major discomfort. I proceeded to flush the remainder of the pills down the toilet. Years later, a member of the crew on this shoot met me for lunch, and he mentioned his observation that I'd been depressed on that trip. Sometimes I hide it well, other times I don't.

Reframing

Following the nasty encounter with Charlie, I descended into a spiral of self-loathing, blaming myself for not maturely handling that brief but painful episode. Looking back, I would have cherished a conversation with one of my former allies to discuss my failure to step up and confront him about his inappropriate behavior. Perhaps a colleague would have challenged my self-blaming with the facts, all of which pointed to an external explanation. This process has been called reframing. To reframe is to see a situation from a different perspective—which is one of the goals of therapy. Stephen Wolin, M.D is a clinical professor of psychiatry, and his wife, Sybil Wolin, Ph.D. is a developmental psychologist. Both are widely published and highly regarded in the fields of mental health and resilience. I came across the following quote from the Wolins, which I found to be extremely insightful *"While you cannot change the past, you can change the way you understand it. You can frame your story around themes of your resilience or themes of your damage. You can find reasons to be proud in some of your worst memories, or you can let yourself be overwhelmed by the harm of it all. Anybody can be a reframer. It's not something that only happens in therapy. The promise of sympathy that comes with a victim's status is enticing bait. But if you take it, you will be helplessly hooked to your pain."*

    Here's how the internal dialogue of reframing might have sounded had I practiced it: "Brad, as you're aware, the company's revenues have been skyrocketing, yet net profits haven't met expectations. Charlie is under pressure from the board to right his ship. His actions towards you were clearly not the actions of the Charlie you've known and trusted all these years. He's got one agenda, and it involves finding the fastest way to create change in his area. This sense of urgency created the conditions for him to lash out at you. You're taking this as a personal attack and aren't considering the context of that meeting. Charlie would love to hear the board say, 'Thank goodness! We've finally got that area of the company streamlined and back to its former outstanding level of service!' Brad, this is about him, not you." Such a reframe of my situation would have enabled me to see more clearly the forces at play that had led to his outburst. This thinking process would have been highly therapeutic. Charlie's actions can't be changed—they happened, and he apologized. Having this skill at the ready would have spared me a great deal of unhappiness.

A Note on Therapy

So far, therapy hasn't been beneficial—which is to say I'm still open to the possibility. That's not to suggest that others don't benefit from talking about their troubles with a skilled professional. I'm aware of many who have experienced significant results from therapy and would never discourage anyone who suffers from pursing this avenue. Experts in the treatment of depression seem to be unanimous that the best approach to finding relief is the combination of antidepressant medication and talk therapy. Of the many types available, cognitive behavior therapy, or CBT, is considered the gold standard. I recently heard that a new therapy called EMDR, which stands for Eye Movement Desensitization and Reprocessing, has been producing impressive results. A knowledgeable person told me about an amazing

The View from Under My Desk

therapist (her words) who practices EMDR and I quickly made an appointment. After several sessions, I wasn't experiencing any relief and terminated that attempt. Therapy just hasn't worked for me—at least not yet. I make that assertion after several failed attempts in seeking out professionals who offered no relief. I confided my troubles to a friend, who recommended a therapist he was seeing. At the time, my daughter was dating a young man who lived next door to the therapist I sought out, who practiced out of her home. With the stigma of mental illness hovering over me, I was afraid his family would recognize my car in her driveway, put two and two together, and determine that I was a head case. But I ratcheted up my courage and drove to her house anyway. The pain demanded some relief. The only takeaway from the many sessions I spent with her was her observation that I didn't have a "buffer" against the slings and arrows of daily life. Perhaps she was telling me I had a pessimistic explanatory style, but I never acquired the skills necessary to help me develop this buffer. I wasn't making progress and decided the to move on, finding a psychiatrist in the Yellow Pages.

At the time, the community I lived in wasn't large. I'd been in a high-profile job and was terrified from the irrational fear of walking into the shrink's office and being recognized, given the stigma that surrounds depression or any mental illness. So my first appointment went unfulfilled as I approached his office, only to turn away in fear of being seen. My next attempt to access this psychiatrist was to call and ask for his last appointment of the day, thinking that the office would be devoid of other patients. Finally, the pain became more than I could bear, and I sucked it up and walked into his office. His assistant had obviously told him of my strategy to avoid being seen because his first question was, "Are you famous?" I had to suppress a laugh. During my first session, I was disappointingly prescribed Prozac. I dutifully took it, with no beneficial effect. At my next appointment, I described a serious lack of energy. The doctor's recommendation was a prescription for the amphetamine Dexedrine, a stimulant used in the '60's as a diet drug, which I'd taken on those drives from college to Sun Valley. The drug over-stimulated my body to the point that I could barely recover from the exhaustion it created. I would leave work at 5pm and go home to lie on my bed. It took until around 9am the next day before I was functional. Though I eventually abandoned them, the stimulation did provide some relief. Years later I returned to Dexedrine, but the anxiety was intolerable, and I eventually settled on one of its cousins, Adderall, a band aid approach that boosts my flagging energy but fails to treat the depressed mood that pervades my life. More about the potential dangers of relying on this drug will be looked at in a later section.

The View from Under My Desk

Chapter 9: Don't Abruptly Stop Taking Your Meds

"Stopping venlafaxine (Effexor) abruptly may result in one or more of the following withdrawal symptoms: irritability, nausea, feeling dizzy, vomiting, nightmares, headache, and/or paresthesias (prickling, tingling sensation on the skin)"
National Alliance on Mental Illness (NAMI)

    Having found no relief from Prozac, an SSRI (selective serotonin reuptake inhibitor), I learned about a new antidepressant in a different classification (an SNRI, or serotonin and norepinephrine reuptake inhibitor), and was soon taking a daily dose of Effexor. Buoyed by the beauties of the surroundings of Vancouver, BC while on a family vacation, I decided I no longer needed Effexor, a disastrous decision made without any knowledge of the potential dangers involved in discontinuing a powerful psychotropic drug.

    During my oldest son's senior year in high school, he announced he wanted me to take him on a ski trip—not just any ski trip. He'd been doing his research, and discovered the largest ski resort in North America, Whistler/Blackcomb, about an hour and half from Vancouver in Canada. It was to be a father/son bonding experience, and at the time, I had the money (along with nothing to do at work) to indulge his fantasy. Our trip was a success, consisting of three consecutive days of hard-core skiing. The runs were much longer than I was used to, but I was still young enough, and in good enough shape to keep up with my 18-year old son. I took my camera and devoted one day to taking shots of Brian flying off jumps. One of these photos still hangs in my house.

I fell in love with the place and vowed to take the rest of my family there. So knowing I wouldn't be missed at work during a week in the summer of '97, I packed up Brian's three younger siblings and along with Debbi, we headed to Vancouver and Whistler. Hang with me because I'm about to describe the hell that occurs when you suddenly stop taking an anti-depressant you've been on for two and half years.

It was summertime, and Whistler boasted some excellent mountain biking trails. Thinking about cruising down this famous mountain seemed irresistible, so I first rented bikes for the family, which consisted of 8-year-old Josh, 13-year-old Brittany, 17-year-old Steven (who, as an independently minded teenager wasn't thrilled to be on a vacation with his family), along with bikes for my wife and myself. The bike rental shop asked for the ages of my family, got us the proper equipment, and it was off to purchase passes to ride the gondola up the mountain. Again, I was asked for age information of those who would be biking.

With excitement running high in anticipation for this outing, we donned our bike helmets, and presented ourselves to the gondola operator at the bottom of the mountain to be whisked to the top for our first ride down. However, I was about to encounter resistance that would reveal the horrors of abruptly stopping Effexor. The young gondola operator sized us up and asked me how old eight-year old Josh was. I immediately went on the defensive, way out of proportion to the situation. I knew why she was asking his age; I guessed correctly that the resort had an age limit that Josh didn't meet. She informed me that he wouldn't be allowed to ride the gondola and bike with the rest of us.

Disaster on the Mountain

I immediately came undone. I angrily explained that both the bike shop and the ticket office had asked for our ages, which I'd provided, and had said nothing about an age requirement. Getting everyone outfitted had taken some doing, and I belligerently explained that there had been two occasions when we should have been told that Josh was too young, yet I'd paid for his bike and ticket, with the full expectation of him participating with the rest of us. She was unmoved by my angry tirade, steadfastly refusing to grant him access to the gondola. At this point, Debbi rationally suggested that she and Josh could bike around the village while the rest of us descended the mountain. In the midst of an Effexor-induced withdrawal, I lost all control. I ignored the gondola attendant and demanded to see a superior, who soon appeared and listened to my highly annoyed explanation of events that had led to that point. She relented, but with a caveat. Her team on the mountain would keep a close watch on Josh, determining his skill level and ability to navigate his way to the bottom. Somewhat satisfied, I agreed, but my nervous system was a wreck.

    Our first descent went off without incident, and Josh performed admirably, as he did on our second run down the mountain. My uncontrolled anger had gotten what I wanted, and as we made our way down the mountain for the third time, we came to a particularly steep section of the trail. I was concerned with our abilities to handle this treacherous looking segment on our bikes and informed my family we'd get off our bikes and walk down this part of the trail.

    Then disaster struck. As we were walking our bikes down this difficult part of the trail, Debbi's foot went out from under her and her entire body weight came crashing down on her ankle. Watching her writhing in tortuous pain, with no help in sight, I felt helpless. We'd later learn that she'd broken her ankle in a particularly painful way. Before long, mountain employees tasked with maintaining order and safety arrived. They called for a vehicle to drive the dirt fire trails, and after what seemed an eternity, a Suburban equipped with a gurney showed up. Debbi was transported to the small hospital at the base of the mountain, and the doctor on duty informed us that her ankle was indeed fractured, would require surgery to repair, but that there were no physicians at this small hospital available to perform the operation.

    The doctor did his best to support the ankle, and prescribed painkillers. So here we were, a thousand miles from home, with a dire medical emergency and no one possessing the expertise to perform the necessary surgery. To make matters

The View from Under My Desk

worse, getting back to a surgeon in Utah was going to become an ordeal. Debbi somehow made it through the night at the motel, at which point we made the arduous four-hour drive to the Seattle airport, having flown there instead of taking the more expensive flight to Vancouver.

I should pause at this point and emphasize the role of Effexor in this debacle. As I would later learn, a person taking this drug, or any psychotropic medication, should be strongly advised by the prescribing physician to not stop taking it without a slow and gradual weaning process. Shrinks call it tapering. Extreme agitation is a common outcome of stopping Effexor, and my out-of-control behavior with the gondola operator was prime evidence of this effect.

A rational person would have accepted the resort's rules, and Debbi and Josh could have enjoyed a pleasant and safe ride around the village, meeting the rest of us for lunch. I had no idea that my embarrassing and destructive behavior resulted from quitting this drug cold turkey. When it had been prescribed, there had been no mention of its dangers if stopped without a gradual reduction in its consumption. Another common side effect from stopping the drug is referred to as "brain zaps" an extremely unpleasant sensation of having one's brain shocked intermittently. These effects can last for days. After two and a half years on this medication, my body had adapted to its effects, and abruptly stopping it led to a ruined vacation, and had left my wife in utter agony.

The mountain biking incident had occurred

on a Friday and our departure from the Seattle airport was scheduled for Sunday. I tried to get an earlier flight, but everything was booked, which meant more misery for Debbi. After enduring almost unbearable pain for two days, we finally boarded the plane. Upon arriving in Salt Lake City, it took several adults to lift my pain-ridden wife into the family van. First thing Monday morning, I called the orthopedic surgeon's office and explained the dire nature of Debbi's situation. Fortunately, a compassionate doctor, upon seeing her injury, scheduled surgery for that very day. She would have two titanium plates inserted, along with ten titanium screws to enable her to heal. The aftermath of the surgery was extremely painful, as Debbi can't take painkillers due to nausea, so the next several days were agony.

Antidepressant Discontinuation Syndrome–Buyer Beware

This event happened almost two decades years ago, and she still has pain in her ankle. And my ignorance about the effects of stopping this drug, which I partially blame the doctor for, cause me to feel guilt anytime she mentions her ankle is bothering her. I also recognize that I could have done my due diligence to learn more about this drug. Fortunately, she doesn't hold me responsible, although I know in my heart I was. But it made me highly aware that psychotropic drugs are to be taken only with a buyer beware mindset, having a full awareness of their side effects and how to stop taking them.

I've since learned that what I was experiencing from abruptly quitting Effexor has a name: Antidepressant Discontinuation Syndrome. In all the years I've tried various antidepressant drugs, no family doctor nor psychiatrist who's prescribed them ever mentioned anything about how to stop taking these medications. This is how one source describes the results of doing so: "venlafaxine (the generic term for the drug I'd been taking–Effexor) seems to be particularly difficult to discontinue, and prolonged withdrawal syndrome (post-acute-withdrawal syndrome, or PAWS) lasting over 18 months has been reported. Sensory and movement disturbances have also been reported, including imbalance, tremors, vertigo, dizziness, and electric-shock-like experiences in the brain, often described by people who have them as "brain zaps." Mood disturbances such as dysphoria (a state of feeling unwell or unhappy, the opposite of euphoria), with a report from the Washington Post indicating that service members with dysphoria are eight times more likely to attempt suicide that other troops. Anxiety, or agitation are also reported, as are cognitive disturbances such as confusion and hyperarousal. A 2009 Advisory Committee to the FDA found that the safety information provided by the manufacturer not only neglected important information about managing discontinuation syndrome, but also explicitly advised against opening capsules, a practice required to gradually taper dosage."

I share this as a warning for anyone either contemplating using antidepressants, as well as for those currently taking them. I am **not** suggesting these medications should be avoided–many struggling with depression have had positive experiences with them, including some who claim their lives were literally saved through their use. What I am attempting to communicate is that this syndrome is real, that I experienced it firsthand (with a horrific outcome, both for myself as well as Debbi), and that patients need to become informed about how to go off these meds if they or their physicians decide this to be the best course of action.

The View from Under My Desk

Chapter 10: Jobless and Aimless

*"The problem was, I had been inadequate all along.
I simply hadn't thought about it."*
Sylvia Plath, The Bell Jar

    I was now thirteen years into my job at the Covey Leadership Center and began to itch for a new experience. I had been granted stock in the company and was wanting to take a brief sabbatical from the work world before diving back in. 1998 arrived, and I decided it was time for a change. I'd had a truly unique and highly satisfying job working with the Seven Habits. I couldn't turn my stock into cash or some type of other investment for two years, but I had enough money set aside that I wasn't feeling any urgency to immediately start earning money in a new job. It appeared on paper that I was financially secure, I had a new country club membership, I had just purchased a high-end luxury car, and the local PBS station had come calling. Would I be interested in producing a series of public service announcements to promote the local university? The topics of the spots seemed interesting, some even dealing with leadership, and I thought this was a gift from heaven, falling into my lap at just the right time. I spent the next several months conducting research for the project, enthusiastically interviewing a variety of professors and starting to see how to create these short videos.
    I hadn't sought out the PBS folks, and I truly believed this was a stroke of luck, since I hadn't contacted this group, enabling me to avoid the

hassles of conducting a job search. But then things turned south; after months of research, my calls to the executive producer, my superior in this case, went unreturned. I was perplexed. He and his boss, the station manager, had seemed so excited to produce and air these spots, and now I couldn't get through to discuss next steps. I vividly recall finally reaching the executive producer during a round of golf. I was on the fifth hole, and my anger and frustration were running high. I can still see my playing partners staring at me in disbelief as I unloaded on this guy. He hadn't had the fortitude to tell me the project had been canned and that my services were no longer required, so he'd put off calling me. So much for good luck. As I reflect on this instance of expectations gone awry, I've asked myself whether I've ever put off speaking with someone when my message was something the other person didn't want to hear? And the answer is an unequivocal yes.

  At the ripe old age of 46, I needed to keep working, regardless of the value of my stock, which turned out to be illusory. Too late to be of help, I would later read an interview in *Golf Digest* by a well-known golfer in the 1950's, a fellow named Jackie Burke, who'd won the Masters, perhaps the most prestigious accomplishment in golf. In a wide-ranging interview, he made the following observation: *"Everybody wants to retire early. Well, I've seen early retirement, and it's not pretty. These 50-year-old guys hang out at the club constantly, because they have nowhere else to go. They get sick of golf; you never see them smiling when they're coming up 18. Don't retire. Leisure time is dangerous. You might wind up inside a bottle of bourbon. You are put on this earth to produce, so get with it."* Wise advise that I wish I'd followed. I didn't wind up inside a bottle of alcohol, but not working would eventually drive me to prescription drug abuse to self-medicate depression and the lack of meaning the absence of work creates.

After leaving Covey, I should have taken Jackie Burke's advice, regardless of how much money I thought I had. Instead, I used my country club membership to maximum effect, practically living at the course. I had an inkling this lifestyle wasn't working when I sat down at my computer after a frustrating round of golf and typed myself a letter. It was titled: Stay off the golf course. In it, I tried to explain to myself that playing golf as much as I was doing was a useless exercise in selfishness and self-absorption. I tried to recount all the miserable rounds of golf I'd played, and how my time at the course wasn't contributing anything of value to anyone.

Serving Others

The principal at the local elementary school must have gotten wind that I had time on my hands, and made a call to Debbi, who'd been a PTA president when our kids attended the school. She mentioned that there was a second grader whose father was in prison, whose mother had abandoned him, that he was being raised by his income-deficient grandmother, had no friends, and was acting out in various ways in the classroom as well as the playground. She wondered if I would be willing to intervene by coming over to the school and having lunch with the boy, whose name was Jonathan. This call occurred almost immediately following my departure from Covey. Debbi relayed the principal's request and having nothing better to do than an occasional ski day, agreed to give it a try.

    I wasn't exactly certain how to bond with a seven-year-old with behavioral problems, so I did the first thing that came to mind. All kids like McDonald's, right? So I showed up in my brand-new Audi, walked into the school, told the secretary about the principal's request that Jonathan and I were to have lunch together, got him checked out, and we were off to McDonald's. The car I picked him up in was fresh off the showroom floor, and Jonathan remarked how the car reminded him of the smell of new clothes. I did my best to bond with the child, we ate lunch, and I returned him to school.

    Then it hit me: I needed to help this kid connect with his peers and taking him away for lunch and missing playground time wouldn't accomplish this. So the next day, I purchased a lunch ticket, was assigned my lunch pass code, and went through the lunch line with Jonathan and all the other children. After the two of us got our lunch trays filled with the delicious fare of an elementary school lunch line, I found a table with kids who looked like they were about Jonathan's age, and started bantering with them while trying to get my young charge involved in the conversation. We next made our way out to the playground, and I initially

The View from Under My Desk

floundered in my efforts to engage him in fun activities. So following lunch the next day, I procured a basketball and we proceeded to play some hoops until the bell rang.

Seeing the needs some of these kids had, I decided to ramp up my volunteer efforts by eating lunch with them and organizing games on the playground. I vowed to get further involved by going into the classrooms of some of the more troubled kids and helping them with their studies. I was shocked to see how these children were being neglected by their parents, and the dismal living conditions they endured as I visited some of their homes.

What's more, I felt good about myself when I engaged with these kids. Sally Brampton described how small acts of service are beneficial to the doer of the deed: *"We expand rather than contract, and so the world expands along with us. We can change our whole day (and other people's) with a single kind word or ruin it by an angry exchange. By thinking outside ourselves, we also stop thinking about how life isn't giving us happiness and how we might give a little happiness to life."* This was a lesson that I would have to learn more than once, but this service certainly helped ease my depression.

Little did I know that another volunteer position was lurking, one that would dramatically change my life, and not all for the better.

Chapter 11: Opiates

"People with family histories of alcoholism tend to have lower levels of endorphins—the endogenous morphine that is responsible for many of our pleasure responses—than do people genetically disinclined to alcoholism. Alcohol will slightly raise the endorphin level of people without the genetic basis for alcoholism; it will dramatically raise the endorphin level of people with that genetic basis. Specialists spend a lot of time formulating exotic hypotheses to account for substance abuse. Most experts point out, strong motivations for avoiding drugs; but there are also strong motivations for taking them. People who claim not to understand why anyone would get addicted to drugs are usually people who haven't tried them or who are genetically fairly invulnerable to them."
— Andrew Solomon, *The Noonday Demon: An Atlas of Depression*

    Hanging out at the country club and volunteering at the elementary school were by now my principal activities in life. A neighbor friend employed by one of the local universities must have observed my routine and thought I could use a bit more meaning in my life. He suggested to a colleague responsible for selecting volunteers for leadership positions of student groups that I might make a good candidate. I was summoned to a meeting with this fellow, who, after informing me of a volunteer's responsibilities, one of which was to get acquainted with the students under their charge

The View from Under My Desk

and refer those who were struggling with various life issues to the appropriate campus resource centers, asked if I would like to become involved. With time on my hands, the opportunity to work with college kids sounded interesting and I agreed to help. Little did I know what I had just signed up for.

My First Interview

With little more than a cursory orientation to this new role, I began my duties during an afternoon in July 1999. The first person I encountered was a tiny wisp of a young woman named Sarah, cute in her pigtails, and dead serious in her demeanor. She walked into my office, took a seat, and before I'd had the chance to exchange pleasantries, such as inquiring about her major, or where she was from, matter-of-factly announced, "My boyfriend and I had oral sex, both ways." Responding with "So—how are your studies going?" didn't seem like the right response. Not yet used to my new leadership position, and never having heard someone make a statement like that, I was completely unprepared for what to say. I managed some type of reply and would go on to learn that this young co-ed had been date raped and was perhaps acting out sexually, although that's strictly speculative. This was to be a crucial and timely interview, as it led me to pursue resources that could be useful to her because of the trauma she'd experienced from the rape and useful in helping other students.

I was aware that the university provided

counseling services to students experiencing mental health concerns, so I asked if she would be willing to speak with a counselor. She flatly refused. To complicate matters, this young woman, who weighed no more than 100 pounds, had been so traumatized by the rape that she was refusing to eat. So there I sat, my first day on the job, trying to figure out how to assist this obviously hurting person, who wasn't pursuing behaviors that were in her best interest. As we talked, she revealed that, in her opinion, the rape investigation had been botched by the university and that the perpetrator had not been disciplined. She was terrified of running into him, forcing her to relive the nightmare he'd created.

During our time together, Sarah mentioned that there had been one person in the university's administration who'd been involved in the rape case that seemed caring and concerned. I asked for his name, and later that week, called him to request that he provide counseling services to Sarah. He informed me that he was strictly an administrator and didn't possess a license to practice therapy. However, he went on to say that he had a friend who was a full-time therapist in the counseling center, that this friend had a personality like his own, and that perhaps Sarah could benefit from seeing him.

At my next meeting with her, I explained the results of my phone call, and asked Sarah if she'd be willing to meet with the therapist. She reluctantly agreed, and I told her I'd make the arrangements. Fearing that she might bolt during the time of her appointment, I conspired with her roommate to ensure she'd be home prior to the appointment. I drove to her apartment, led her to my car, and walked her into the counselor's office. After ensuring she hadn't run out, I waited for the appointment to conclude, after which I drove her to a nutritionist's office with the hope that she could receive some help with her eating disorder.

This experience with Sarah was pivotal as numerous students came to me with mental health issues. Through this and other experiences, I learned that most volunteer leaders, when dealing with a student's mental health concerns, would simply advise them to go to the counseling center. This approach would typically lead to one of two outcomes: either the student wouldn't go at all, or they would show up and be assigned to a graduate student, rather than a full-fledged licensed therapist, who was essentially practicing on the students. These encounters were often less than satisfactory, given the grad student's limited experience. So early on in my efforts to secure competent mental health services for these students, I researched the therapists in the counseling center. Who was good with eating disorders? Who was especially competent in depression? Who could help a girl who was cutting herself? It was only after doing my due diligence on the university's therapists that I would call, make the appointment, and then follow-up with the student to determine the results. And my own experiences with depression were paying off—I was much more sensitive to these stigmatized issues given the experiences I'd had.

From mid 1999 to the end of 2000, I thought I'd found my place in life. I was spending large amounts of time helping at-risk elementary students, I played a good deal of golf, owned a lot of Covey stock, I felt my family life was solid, I was heavily engaged with the university students, and I was temporarily giving depression the slip. It was not to last. One day as I was watching my son Josh play soccer in the summer of 2000, I got a call from the person who'd built my house. He was hitting up "wealthy" former customers, asking for money for which he was prepared to pay an outrageous interest rate. It sounded too good to be true, so I consulted my then financial adviser, who told me it looked good and to go for it. That single decision would prove devastating.

An Attack and its Aftermath

Throughout my first year and a half as a volunteer leader, I'd noticed a young woman named Susan who didn't seem to care for me, despite my repeated attempts to include her in key meetings and going out of my way to thank her for services she provided to members of our group. I'd heard she didn't think I was effective in my duties, and I tried reaching out to her, hoping for an appointment to clear the air. But when my assistant would call to arrange a meeting, she would invariably refuse to agree to an appointment. I tried calling myself, but she wouldn't come to the phone. Susan was a regular attender of group social gatherings, so following one such event, I literally ran after her, hoping to corral her in hopes of setting up a meeting. But she ran faster.

The View from Under My Desk

Through persistence and patience, I finally got her to agree to meet with me. I was a bit nervous, having heard of her distaste for my approach to running the group, but I told myself I had to resolve this; I couldn't have a group member holding me in contempt. As the interview began, I could tell it wasn't going to end well. When I asked her to describe her concerns, the floodgates opened, and a tirade gushed out of her mouth.

She began by declaring that I was a fake and a fraud, and had no business being in a leadership role, as I was clearly ineffective in my actions, and cited as evidence mistakes she believed I'd made in carrying out my assignment. By now, I was reeling from her verbal onslaught and could barely think of what to say next. Finally, she produced a four-page, handwritten single spaced letter, laying out in minute detail my failings as a person and as a leader. One of my worst mistakes had been the time I publicly thanked her for baking some pies for a group activity. Unknown to me, this had caused her deep embarrassment and further validated her strongly held view that I was less than worthless as a leader.

I would learn too late that she had a history of hating any male figure in authority over her, had been raised by an abusive step-father who told her she was too ugly to ever get a date, and had been verbally abusive to numerous roommates she'd had during the four years she'd lived in her apartment.

Half-believing the ugly comments she made on that awful afternoon, I was further shocked when she simply got up and walked out, leaving me holding a letter that I knew would be full of vile statements about me and my unfitness for the job. I had several more interviews scheduled that afternoon. Reeling from the encounter, I muddled through the next two, but then informed my assistant that I wasn't feeling well and asked him to reschedule the remaining interviews. I drove home in a state of utter despair.

I was experiencing some of the worst emotional pain of my life. For a year and a half, I had poured myself into this role with everything I had, giving countless hours to the care of this group of students. There had been numerous fun times, and the volunteer leader to whom I reported would sing my praises at our monthly meetings. Now I was being told by someone I'd tried to befriend that I was a worthless, unworthy piece of garbage who had no business being in my role.

This horrific interchange took place in January 2001. We'd had an early snow that previous fall, and in preparing my John Deere riding mower to become a snowplow, I'd tweaked my back, and the pain was severe enough that I made an appointment to see that friendly PA. He prescribed sixty Percocet, a powerful and addictive opiate-based painkiller, along with a similar number of muscle relaxers. The pain eventually subsided, and after taking one of each, I tucked them away in my briefcase and forgot about them.

But the need for relief from the horrendous interview jogged my memory, at which point I drove home, took out the pills, and downed two of each. The relief I experienced from self-medicating my mental anguish was almost instantaneous. Suddenly,

The View from Under My Desk

all was right with the world, and the sting of this young woman's remarks, along with her complaints against me written out in a carefully worded letter, went blissfully away. What I didn't know at that moment was that I'd made a serious mistake, one that would lead me into a downward spiral, courtesy of opiate-based painkillers.

The day following the personal attack, not thinking of any long-term consequences, I downed more drugs, trying to kill the pain of my encounter with Susan and setting myself up for drug dependence.

The drugs became part of my routine, which I increasingly needed just to make it through the day. I was still able to discharge my leadership duties, as I wasn't taking large amounts and therefore remained functional. But I definitely needed them to cope. On one of my visits to the PA to get my prescription refilled for "back pain" he confided in me that he'd become an addict, that at the height of his addiction he was taking thirty pills a day, was in recovery, had lost his license, but was now back in the saddle. This should have been a warning, but I thought that my two pills a day regime was innocuous, and he continued to supply me with the opiates.

Ignoring a Wakeup Call

One day in March of that year, I had just finished conducting a group meeting. Like I mentioned, I could function just fine, and no one was the wiser. As I was packing up my things to begin interviews, a young man approached me in a state of despair. He needed to see me, and he needed to see me right now. As we entered my office and I closed the door, I said, "You want to kill yourself, don't you?" During a get-to-know you interview at the beginning of the semester, he'd confided that his father, a former Marine, had constantly belittled and abused him for not being macho enough to fit his father's expectations. He then went on to describe a suicide attempt he'd made that summer, which was thankfully thwarted when an astute friend caught him just in time.

    I spent the next two hours on the phone with a therapist, who got this suicidal student admitted to the psychiatric unit at the local hospital. That night, I paid him a visit in the locked ward, being admitted only because I was his campus leader. While waiting to see him, I absent-mindedly picked up some literature in the waiting room. In the brochure I was perusing, I read that the combination of opiate-based painkillers like the ones I was taking daily, combined with muscle relaxers constituted the equivalent of heroin. Another wake-up call ignored.

    I spent the next two and half years dependent on these drugs. To be clear, I never doctor-shopped, I never stole a prescription pad, and I never broke the law. I simply had a medical professional willing to dispense these pills for my so-called back pain in large quantities. Ironically, I would later learn that one of the symptoms of detoxing from opiates whenever I'd run out is severe lower back pain, but not knowing that, and cycling on and off these drugs, I was in an out of the offices of back specialists and pain clinics. Nothing structural could be found—I

The View from Under My Desk

was undergoing the body's natural response to withdrawing from narcotics.

During this period, I spent my daytime hours in isolation, holed up in an office with no co-workers, no boss, no peers, no one reporting to me—no one. I believe the lack of regular human connection played a huge role in my use of drugs to numb the pain of this paucity of human interaction and contributed to a deepening depression. If you listen to or watch TED talks, this problem, along with its solution, is discussed in *Everything You Think You Know About Addiction is Wrong*, and the speaker ends with this thought, *"The opposite of addiction isn't sobriety, the opposite of addiction is connection."* Solomon also addresses the need for depressives to experience connection with others by noting that *"depression is a disease of loneliness, and substantial evidence holds that informed human contact is among its best solutions. The perception that someone is paying attention to what you are experiencing is greatly reassuring."* This quote from Sally Brampton provides useful advice for those living with and around depressives, *"I believe, completely, that life is about connection; that nothing else truly matters. People often say, 'I don't know how to help.' This is one way—through empathy but more importantly, through connection. Don't think, as so many people do, that depressives are best left alone. They are not. Ignoring or dismissing depression only makes it worse. It never makes it better."* Pg. 102 Shoot the Damn Dog. Regardless of whatever amount of money my dwindling portfolio contained, I needed to find a job that would provide me with connections to people.

Unused Strategies—Opportunities Missed

Most people who experience an attack on their self-worth don't resort to narcotics to cope with whatever emotional pain they may experience. Susan's vitriol would have been the perfect opportunity to apply one or more of the coping strategies I've discussed so far. For example, the Seligman application is clear: I had just been informed I was worthless (personal), that everything I'd done as a leader had been futile (pervasive), and that I was irredeemable (permanent). And I'd bought it all. I wish that someone, perhaps that leader, had helped me reframe the experience and practice learned optimism.

Or I could have employed Dr. Ellis' ABCDE model of rational thinking, perhaps with the help of another person who recognized my distress. Instead of allowing Susan's words to pierce me to the core, I could have disputed any irrational beliefs they caused by reminding myself of all the good I'd accomplished in this role—tangible results reported to me by therapists I'd referred students to, my own supervisor, and the students themselves. Another rational belief leading to a healthier consequence would have been to tell myself that this was one person's opinion, strong as it was, and there were 150 other students who would have vigorously disagreed with her.

Chapter 12: Rudderless

"Without purpose and meaning in our lives, we banish ourselves to wander this plane of existence with self-destructive tendencies until the bell tolls and our breath capsizes in our lungs, snatching our chance to redeem ourselves forever."
— A.J. Darkholme, *Rise of the Morningstar*

My use of painkillers, combined with the lack of a job, turned out to be a disastrous combination. Research has shown that one of the top risk factors for addiction is joblessness. The drugs would mask my depression for a time, but then it would worsen. By now, I was becoming more severely depressed as the opiates were losing their effectiveness, my stock was dropping like a rock and I remained unemployed. I continued my volunteer role, but I made an appointment with my superior, and gave him the bad news: I was having a harder and harder time discharging my duties due to depression. He listened carefully, and with all good intentions, tried to cheer me up by telling me what a stellar job I was doing. I managed to muddle through one more year, a shell of my former, enthusiastic self, at which point I resigned this volunteer post.

The Pills Lose Their Magic

At that point, having no job and nothing to do, Debbi became alarmed at my stagnant status. At the age of 51, life looked bleak. I continued to cycle on and off the opiates, but they had lost their magic.

One day following the termination of my volunteer role at the university, I took nine pills, by far the most I'd ever consumed in one day. The effect was negligible. My days of finding relief from treatment-resistant depression through narcotics were over.

Though I don't compare myself to William Styron the writer, we both had the same experience in failing to find relief from substances that once granted us respite from the pain of depression. Styron relied on alcohol throughout his adult life. But once he turned sixty, the drug lost its magical powers. He describes his experiences with alcohol's failure to tamp down his pain as betrayal. *"It struck me quite suddenly, almost overnight: I could no longer drink. It was as if my body had risen up in protest, along with my mind, and had conspired to reject this daily mood bath which it had so long welcomed and, who knows? perhaps even come to need."* I was having a similar experience with opiates, those once magical pills that offered almost instantaneous relief from the pain of depression.

About this time, depression had worsened to the point that I once again decided to seek psychiatric assistance, in spite of my prior experience. I decided to call the hospital, thinking that shrinks there who dealt with the truly insane in the psych ward would possess the expertise to alleviate my suffering. The psychiatrist I was assigned reminded me of a nerdy math professor. I had assumed, wrongly as it turned out, that professionals in the mental health arena possess excellent social skills.

After introducing myself, my new friend

turned to his computer and began asking me a series of questions, never making eye contact, let alone attempting to put me at ease in this fraught situation. After answering several of his questions, I was about to erupt with something like, "Did it ever occur to you that people seeking your services might expect just a little human warmth?" But I restrained myself and waited for him to finally turn to me with his recommendation. He handed me two prescriptions, with no explanation of what either was intended to treat.

But being in pain can be a strong motivator, despite a pathetically conducted psychiatric evaluation. I drove to the pharmacy and paid for my drugs: Provigil and Depakote. After choking on the costs of these pills intended to relieve my suffering, I went home to see what I could learn about them online. Provigil is intended to promote "wakefulness" and is prescribed to narcolepsy sufferers. Depakote is a mood-stabilizer used to treat individuals with bi-polar disorder. I was dubious: I didn't have narcolepsy, nor had I battled bi-polar issues. But I dutifully took them with zero benefits for my time, trouble, and money. I tried to give the wakefulness and bi-polar drugs a chance to do work their magic. But it wasn't to be. There weren't any side effects, but neither was there any relief from the pain.

Chapter 13: The Promise of a New Treatment

"Today expect something good to happen to you no matter what occurred yesterday. Realize the past no longer holds you captive. It can only continue to hurt you if you hold on to it. Let the past go. A simply abundant world awaits."
— Sarah Ban Breathnach, *Simple Abundance: A Daybook of Comfort and Joy*

It was now 2003, I was five years out of the workforce, I had managed to connect with several worthless financial advisors, all of whom lost my money while they collected their fees, and my stock was in a free fall. I needed a job, and I needed one desperately. So I prepared my resume, went online at various job search sites, uploaded my credentials, and waited for the phone to ring with attractive job offers. But the phone was silent. My missives had gone into the black hole of the Internet, and I was clueless as to why I, as a previously successful training and development professional, couldn't even conjure up an interview. The office I inhabited at that time had no window, so I had the perfect space for my depressed episodes, turning off the light, wadding up a sweater for a pillow, and lying on the floor, trying to unsuccessfully battle the demons that haunted me.

One early morning in April of that year, I couldn't sleep, so I went out to the living room to lie on the couch, contemplating the mess I was in. And then it hit me: the films I'd produced for Covey were now about ten years old. What if I could reconnect with my friend, the director, and we'd do a new round? With our previous track record, how could the organization say no? I'd simply ask for a meeting with Stephen, who loved the films and used them in all his speeches and present my can't-say-no proposal. I'd be back in the saddle and the good times would once again roll. But times had changed. Whereas I had once enjoyed almost limitless access to Stephen, I was now shunted off to one of his many minions, who agreed to meet with me.

It turned out that the organization now contracted out all its media work to a studio, run by a young man who had previously reported to me. My timing was good, I was told, because new media was in the works and my director and I would be among several production teams assigned to produce various videos. From a work standpoint, what could be more dispiriting that having once controlled a budget of several hundred thousand dollars, to now scoring a part-time assignment being directed by a former underling? In the end, my director friend and I did sign on to help produce a total of three short films, but the halcyon days of running the show were over.

Transcranial Magnetic Stimulation

Sometime in late 2004, I heard about a new depression treatment, called repetitive transcranial magnetic stimulation (rTMS). It supposedly produced the benefits of electro-convulsive therapy (ECT), but without its troubling side effects. I'd read about ECT in a book called *Shock: The Healing*

Power of Electroconvulsive Therapy, written by the wife of the former Democratic presidential candidate, Michael Dukakis. Mrs. Dukakis had a history of self-medicating her depression with a combination of alcohol and amphetamines, and she claimed that ECT had literally saved her life. It was a compelling argument, especially in light of my earlier and somewhat positive exposure to amphetamines in college. Maybe Kitty Dukakis and I shared similar brain chemistries.

But I wasn't ready to go all in with ECT. It's highly stigmatized and the more I read about it, the more appealing this new alternative seemed. As I researched rTMS, I discovered it was still in its infancy and had yet to be approved by the FDA. rTMS utilizes an electromagnet placed on the scalp that generates magnetic field pulses roughly the strength of an MRI scan. The clinic's brochure outlined the procedure: A physician administered the treatments, which lasted approximately twenty minutes each, twice daily for a minimum of two weeks. The only way to receive the treatment was to travel to Canada, where forward thinking psychiatrists were administering it and studying its effects. At the time, I still had the financial ability to afford the expenses and costs of the procedure, so with great anticipation, I found myself in downtown Vancouver, eagerly, but with some apprehension, awaiting my turn under the magnet.

I recall a brief conversation I had with 14-year-old Josh as we drove home from soccer before I left on my two-week journey that afternoon. I asked him if he knew what depression was. He replied that it's when someone is sad. I told him that I was having difficulties in shaking off this sadness and would be leaving that day to receive treatment. In anticipation of my stay in Canada, Debbi had asked each of my children to write a letter expressing their hopes that the treatment would work. They also expressed their love for me. I was instructed not to open these until I'd arrived, and found them to be very touching, as each of my children wished me the best. This was a highly experimental process, and I was rolling the dice. But with twenty-five years of failed drug therapies, and wanting to avoid ECT, I ponied up the significant amount of cash and was off to Vancouver.

On that first Monday morning, all the patients were given a brief orientation, after which we were asked to complete a depression survey. This would be the baseline against which our treatments would be measured. My score showed definite signs of depression, but I'd managed to fly to Seattle, rent a car, find my way to my hotel in downtown Vancouver, and present myself for treatment the next day. I was functional, but depression was my constant companion.

After the first couple of days, the doctor determined that I was improving. I believe it was his desire to see change, more than anything that was occurring with my mood. Each day I called my wife, as I knew she was eager to hear of any progress. I tried to sound upbeat, even though the treatments weren't lifting my mood.

It was not to be. In spite of the brochure's promises, the doctor's optimism, my wife's hopes, and my own intense desire to experience a lift in mood, nothing changed. I'd arrived full of anticipation for this ECT-like procedure and had spent upwards of $15,000. Disappointedly, I had exhausted yet another approach to alleviating what was becoming a never-ending battle with this unseen beast.

My options were running out, having used every anti-depressant the professionals could throw at me, including some of the earliest created, which are rarely prescribed because of their unpleasant side effects. So I returned from Canada totally disheartened. Still unemployed, still losing large sums of money in the stock market, I went back to closing my office door with the light turned out, curled up on the floor with door locked—not that anyone came calling—lying on my rolled-up sweatshirt.

I continued to apply for jobs online, eventually determining that these sites are completely worthless, at least for me. I can't help but think my depression influenced my joblessness. This statement from a blog summed up my dilemma:

"We also examined how depressed employees fare at different points in the business cycle. It turns out that during robust macroeconomic times, depressed people tend to be highly employable. But when a cyclical downturn occurs–as was the case during the recent Great Recession–employees with depression tend to be disproportionately adversely affected. Not only are they more likely to lose their jobs than their non-depressed counterparts, but part-time work is

The View from Under My Desk

not as widely available." Scientific American Guest Blog, February 25, 2015.

Chapter 14: Getting a Real Job

"All of the great leaders have had one characteristic in common: it was the willingness to confront unequivocally the major anxiety of their people in their time. This, and not much else, is the essence of leadership." — John Kenneth Galbraith

In one cogent sentence, Mr. Galbraith has captured the substance of what it means to be a leader. Toward the end of 2005, I was about to gain a painful lesson in the special hell of anxiety an employee can suffer from problems of leadership. A call came out of the blue, offering me a job, a real job, with a decent salary, benefits, and an office at a company with a solid history of success. The small firm I had worked for years earlier after moving to Utah had morphed into a force to be reckoned with in the training world. Would I like to come onboard and join them in their mission to impact corporate cultures through more effective interpersonal communications? There was a cursory interview with one of the owners, but it was clear the job was mine if I wanted it. One of the founders held my training skills in high regard, and thought I was just what they needed to help their clients learn to be better trainers.

I would last just short of two years in a job with great pay, profit sharing, stock ownership possibilities, some really competent and fun to work with colleagues, and all this with a company leading

The View from Under My Desk

the industry in its field. Having been so unsuccessful during previous years of job searching, how could I not have made this my permanent home?

Trying to Adapt to a New Culture

The answers were complex, and at the time, created a source of tremendous stress and anxiety. This was a training company and having been out of the formal workforce for 8 years, my confidence in my ability to stand in front of a room and present this company's somewhat difficult to deliver (for me at least) curriculum was diminished. Instead of jumping in and volunteering for training assignments, I was holding back, afraid of failing and being labeled unfit for the job. I blame myself for not diving headfirst into the company's training rotation, preferring the safer approach of hiding out in administrative duties. And a depressed mind, coupled with skills that had eroded from lack of use was a bad combination. I would have done well to have heeded the words of a Neil Young song: "It's better to burn out than it is to rust."

With my lack of confidence, I particularly wanted the validation that comes from recognition for my contributions, which I hoped to make. All four of the founders had been colleagues of mine at former employers. This new company had evolved significantly from the program I'd instituted in the lumber industry, courtesy of the Stamford, CT, based consulting firm. Almost thirty years on, my

employer's product was vastly superior to the
program I'd used in the lumber mills.

    All credit for the evolution and improvements
from those early days in the late'70s goes to its
founders, but I couldn't help but think that my
inviting the Stanford research team—which included
one of the founders—into the forest products
industry had been part of the genesis for what had
become this highly sought after training curriculum.
This hit me firmly in the face during days two and
three on the job. The firm's "master trainers,"
independent contractors who sold and trained in their
respective geographic territories, had been invited to
a two day conference to share best practices and to
receive instruction from the founders. As the new kid
on the block, I was clueless about company politics,
which quickly changed. The meeting got underway,
and the four founders, three of whom were former
colleagues from the Covey organization, weren't
referred to by their names. Instead, this elite group,
with whom I'd once been a peer, were now "the
authors." The master trainers seemed to deify them.
They had become gods, yet these were folks I'd once
hobnobbed with. I had introduced one of them, the
lead author of their best-selling book, to the very
approach that had created their status and wealth. As
the master trainers hung on their every word, I
wanted to jump up and scream, "Wait a minute! I
introduced one of your authors to some of the basic
ideas you're all making handsome livings from!
Don't I get at least a little credit?" I withheld giving
voice to that highly immature thought–a thought that

The View from Under My Desk

demonstrated my need for some type of validation. But knowing that my former associates had built a training juggernaut in part from those early beginnings in Oregon was clear every time these four founders were referred to as the authors. This was another reminder of how far I'd fallen. Their productivity and success, which occurred during my many attempts at trying to ride out my depressive episodes, was jolting. I'd been lying on the floor in a darkened office while others were busily and productively engaged in creating something of value.

I find this quotation by Andrew Solomon so descriptive of the depression I've experienced that I've chosen to use it twice in this book: *"The most important thing to remember about depression is this: you do not get the time back. It is not tacked on at the end of your life to make up for the disaster years. Whatever time is eaten by a depression is gone forever. The minutes that are ticking by as you experience the illness are minutes you will not know again."* The minutes had indeed ticked by as I had lain on the floor, causing formerly held skills to atrophy as I fell further behind in the professional world.

During the good years at the Covey Leadership Center, I enjoyed almost unlimited autonomy and had become accustomed to a freewheeling environment, one that enabled me to pursue avant-garde product development efforts that consistently paid off. As I began working at this new role with this new company, I experienced another jolt, encountering an organizational culture that was anything but receptive to change. For instance, I quickly became aware that many clients perceived delivering the company's training to their organizations to be fraught with difficulties. This information wasn't a secret—an internal survey confirmed this. I decided to investigate, attending a program conducted by the company's premier trainer. During the course, an attendee, a woman working for a high tech company in the Silicon Valley, raised her hand and asked an insightful question. "What's your attrition rate with the trainers who return to their organizations, tasked with conducting this program?" she asked. Intrigued, I approached her during a break and asked what lay behind her question. She explained that her CEO had become enamored of the course content by reading the book, had sent her to become certified to train it upon returning home, and proceeded to describe that, as a professional trainer, she would do as asked, but that she experienced the training to be difficult to deliver.

  Armed with this and stories of trainer attrition, which were costly to the company, I proposed investigating the issue of dilemmas trainers faced in presenting the course. After much questioning and resistance ("We've never flown any of our people out to observe clients—why are we spending money on this now?"), I finally received permission to travel to a handful of client sites with the intent of observing client trainers in action, followed by interviewing them to determine their experiences and

The View from Under My Desk

overall satisfaction as internal trainers. I wanted to observe client trainers in their own environments, hoping to observe firsthand how the curriculum actually played out once trainers left the safe confines of being mentored by the training company's master trainers.

As I sat in the back of the room and witnessed these on-site trainings, I was struck by how far afield from the intended deliveries some of these events had become. Upon returning to the home office, I reported my findings but they seemed to fall on deaf ears. After all, the training was award winning, the company was hugely successful financially, and there seemed no reason to change, other than the fact that large numbers of would-be trainers weren't purchasing training materials and conducting courses. Frustrated, I recommended making some simple changes to the trainer manual to facilitate ease of delivery. Again, my suggestions were brushed off. My failure to convince the powers that be to examine their own research and to take my observations and recommendations seriously led to a feeling of powerlessness and impotence. From a depressive point of view, I was having a difficult time feeling that my particular role was necessary. I craved to matter, but felt like the culture, systems, and structures of this organization were sacrosanct, not to be meddled with. To be sure, the founders and senior managers had built a highly profitable and influential business. But the prevailing ethos seemed to be "if it ain't broke, don't fix it." Sebastian Junger, author of *Tribe—On Homecoming and*

Belonging, notes that *"humans don't mind hardship, in fact they thrive on it; what they mind is not feeling necessary. Modern society has perfected the art of making people not feel necessary. It's time for that to end."* I've lived through many days in various jobs I've held not feeling necessary. Any leader who ignores Junger's observation and fails to create conditions whereby his or her people feel essential will pay a price eventually. Feeling vital and being necessary go hand in hand, and savvy managers have their radar attuned to the extent workers see their efforts as essential to team and organization goals.

Having gone to the effort and expense of researching the ways trainers were experiencing delivering the program, and having my findings dismissed so casually, I felt like little I did mattered, that the extent of my control was negligible. In his book *Good Boss, Bad Boss*, Stanford's Bob Sutton, prolific author of management books and professor of management science, elaborates on the importance of feeling in control: *"…study after study shows that when people experience some control over their lives, they enjoy better physical and mental health. Even when people can't control their ultimate fates, their well-being improves when they can influence some aspects of their lives. For bosses, this means your dirty work will do less harm if you can give people some control over when and how bad things happen to them."* My well-being, already on shaky ground, took another hit following my initiative to make a difference for trainers confronted with a difficult to navigate manual. No one in the

The View from Under My Desk

organization was purposefully trying to impede my mental health, but that's how it played out in this instance.

Although I didn't have the opportunity to see my proposal implemented, I later heard from company insiders that my efforts had been the one component behind a revamped manual, which was perceived by clients as less intimidating, facilitating more purchases, more trainings, and increased revenues. I took a small measure of satisfaction in learning that my initiative in seizing a degree of control had paid off. Feelings of hopelessness and helplessness are classic symptoms of depression and were exacerbated by the organization's unwillingness to examine its flagship program. Unfortunately, the sense that the company was pleased with the status quo did not bode well for my need to feel a modicum of control while employed there.

Chapter 15: Another startup and The Next Miracle Cure

"That's the thing about depression: A human being can survive almost anything as long as she sees the end in sight. But depression is so insidious, and it compounds daily, that it's impossible to ever see the end. The fog is like a cage without a key." Elizabeth

    In casting about for a new job, one call led to another, and I ended up learning that a former colleague at Covey had started up a business that included himself and two other founders. Without doing much due diligence on this venture, and strongly driven by my desperation to find a new employer, I jumped ship to what would turn out to be a questionable and unstable business venture. But at that point, I didn't care. This virtual organization offered me a position and a salary, and I announced my departure from my current employer.
    I have a friend whose business at the time included a small warehouse with a cubicle in the far corner. Not wanting to work from home, I asked if I could occupy this Spartan space, which was the most bare bones office facility imaginable. In this isolated space, I could once again be free to stare up at the underside of my desk without being noticed.
As I sat in this desolate locale, I tried not to think of my former well-appointed office at Covey, along with an assistant next door to do my every bidding. I'd fallen far, yet I had a job, however sketchy, they were paying me, and I'd escaped the micromanaging boss, so all was not as grim as my warehouse/office

surroundings would have suggested. A definite downside to this new enterprise, in addition to its less-than-promising business model, is that it was truly virtual; I had no one within physical proximity to talk to. I was also the only person in the company to be performing my job of curriculum design, and having no one with whom to collaborate, proved a lonely existence. Solomon asserts that depression is a disease of loneliness. Working in isolation for me was a definite risk factor for depression.

    At about this same time, I'd learned about a series of clinical trials that were being conducted at the University of Utah medical center, an hour's drive away. The procedure that was being evaluated is called vagus nerve stimulation, which the Mayo Clinic describes as a procedure that *"stimulates the vagus nerve with electrical impulses. Vagus nerve stimulation can be used to treat epilepsy when other treatments haven't worked. Vagus nerve stimulation is also a treatment for depression, and it's being studied for conditions such as multiple sclerosis, migraine and Alzheimer's disease. There's one vagus nerve on each side of your body, running from your brainstem through your neck to your chest and abdomen. With vagus nerve stimulation, a device is surgically implanted under the skin on your chest. A wire is threaded under your skin connecting the device to the left vagus nerve. When activated, the device sends electrical signals along the vagus nerve to your brainstem, which then sends signals to certain areas in your brain."* As with ECT, medical science didn't know how the procedure reduced depressive symptoms, in the cases when, in fact, that occurred.

    A short story on the local news featured the university's venture into clinical trials with vagus nerve stimulation as a treatment for depression. Doctors working with epileptics had noticed that some patients who'd undergone this surgical procedure had become less depressed, leading the business-minded folks at the company that manufactured the device to seek alternative sources of revenue, if the procedure could be shown to lessen depressive symptoms. Here was a clinical trial practically in my backyard, and I was certain I could prove a worthy candidate, given the failure of all the antidepressants I'd tried. So after several trips to be evaluated by those charged with admitting patients into the trial, and using my best persuasive skills, I was in. Even with this seemingly good news, I wanted to know how serious a surgery I was getting myself into. So I met with a nurse, who explained it wasn't major surgery, nor was it minor surgery. But implanting a pulse-generator into my chest and running an electrode up my vagus nerve was still significant surgery. I don't know much about anatomy, but when I learned the vagus nerve was in close proximity to the carotid artery, I got a bit nervous. It seemed that a slight slip of the scalpel would spell disaster.

    But the surgery was successful, insofar as implanting the pulse generator, and connecting the electrode to my vagus nerve. I still had to wait for everything to heal before the device could be activated. Recovery was much worse than expected. I was in serious pain and confined to my house for several days while the incision healed.

      This must have been hell on my wife, seeing her husband undergo yet another treatment promising to alleviate the depression she'd been living with all those years. Depression affects everyone within the sufferer's sphere, especially family members who are forced to tolerate constant moodiness, along with refusals to participate in normal activities, like vacations, and simply hanging out in the backyard after dinner on a Sunday afternoon. I've experienced a great deal of guilt from opportunities I've kept my wife from participating in, and I regret my often sullen demeanor in her presence. Many divorces occur as a result of this disease, with the caregiver finally saying, Enough! But she's hung in there and says she knows there's a different person inside me, once seen and enjoyed. It must be those memories that help her through the hellishness I've put her through.

But Would it Work?

      After waiting for my wounds to heal, I was ushered into the office of a graduate student. This young man, who possessed no medical training, proceeded to turn on the pulse generator, which was initially set at a low voltage to allow me to adapt to the sensation it created. I was in for a shock, literally. Even at the lowest voltage possible, the pulse generator sent a signal to the vagus nerve every 30 seconds, each lasting about five seconds. During that time, speech was forced and difficult, and anyone who knew my normal voice would have asked what was wrong. But I chalked it up to just being part of the deal and went ahead for the next couple of weeks feeling like I was being mildly strangled every thirty seconds. The brochure I'd been given prior to the surgery listed hoarseness, changes in voice and speech, and throat and neck pain as side effects. It didn't mention the sensation of partial strangulation.

At my next appointment, the pulse generator was set even higher. Now there was a definite feeling of discomfort when it went off, and the sensation of being choked was more pronounced. I was given a magnet and told I could eliminate the pulses if they became too uncomfortable, by holding it over the place on my upper chest where the device had been implanted. I found myself making up various excuses when people would ask me what was wrong with my voice. During my weekly visits to the University of Utah's Mood Disorder Clinic (I'd never thought about it that way, but I definitely had a mood disorder), I was asked to complete a questionnaire designed to assess the efficacy of the implant. Unfortunately, nothing positive showed up, but I had endured enough inconvenience from all the trips to the university, along with the pain from the surgery, that I wasn't going to have the device turned off. Perhaps an increase in its voltage would be the silver bullet, in spite of the discomfort to my throat, and the embarrassment I'd endure every thirty seconds during a conversation.

My new "virtual job" consisted of a weekly conference call with all the players, who were located in diverse cities, some overseas. During these calls, I'd hold the magnet over the pulse generator in order to avoid the grabbing feeling around my throat.

Reality Sinks In

  One of the principals of this new business I worked for resided overseas and wanted to meet me over the course of what would become five days of torture, primarily from the pain of the unhealed incision. The trip took place shortly after the surgery, and the doctor advised against making this lengthy journey after such a short recovery period. But the owner was on a tight schedule, and business being business, I got on a plane and made the trip, the slit in my throat where the electrode had been inserted was still raw and bleeding—which my host would ask me about. I made up some kind of story about an injury and he seemed satisfied.
  Since my departure from my previous job, I'd continued to have difficulty sleeping, and had gone back to Ambien, which I'd been taking for daytime anxiety—a use of the drug any doctor would have frowned upon. I knew better. An article in *Sports Illustrated* profiled the career of a well-known golfer from the '60's, a pro by the name of Al Geiberger. This successful touring professional, known as Mr. 59 for his improbable feat of being the first PGA golfer to ever shoot that magical score in a competitive round, had fallen on hard times. Now in his twilight years, he'd endured one setback after another, including two divorces, culminating in the drowning of his 2-year old son. These were followed by a stint in rehab for addiction to Ambien and

painkillers at the Betty Ford Clinic. I knew I was dancing on the edge with my Ambien use and prior dependence on opiates. But such is the lot of someone who's tried all the standard treatments, along with procedures like rTMS and vagus nerve stimulation, all to no avail.

    The flight to my new bosses' homeland was just under 22 hours, scheduled to arrive at 6am. I was exhausted after failing to sleep on the flight. My plan had been to sleep as much as possible on the plane, aided by the little white pills in my briefcase, but flying and sleeping on international trips had never worked for me. I showed up in the early morning hours on his doorstep, having no sleep under my belt. Being utterly exhausted from the sleepless flight, combined with the after effects of my recent surgery presented me with less than ideal conditions to meet and undertake morning to night work sessions.

    I somehow survived the trip yet became highly dismayed at the lack of what I perceived to be a lack of meaningful content this individual and his two partners had generated, which I was expected to convert into a profitable training business. Having been involved in successful training ventures, I saw little upon which to build a curriculum—my assessment was there were few big ideas. In contrast, upon first encountering *The Seven Habits,* I was absolutely convinced of its potential for making an enormous impact. Such was not my impression as I was introduced to the material forming the basis of

The View from Under My Desk

this new venture. This realization was troubling, and the anxiety it created led me to my old habit of using Ambien during the days I was there. I looked for any potential in the so-called intellectual property of this group, but my gut was telling me there was little there. Later in the week, other members of the company arrived, and the atmosphere was festive. On my final night there, a dinner was held, and the mood couldn't have been more upbeat as the conversation flowed freely. Seeing no cause for optimism, I remained mute throughout the gathering.

Upon returning home, I repaired to my Spartan, warehouse office quarters, doing my best to develop a curriculum, and continuing to struggle with finding anything compelling in this content. More than once, with depression raging, I resorted to my practice of crawling under my desk.

Chapter 16: Electroconvulsive Therapy: Going for the Gold Standard

"It was one of the most difficult things I have ever done in my life. I have memory problems as a residual of it; however, I'm alive. That was the main point."
— Kitty Dukakis (wife of 1988 Democratic Presidential Nominee, Michael Dukakis), *Shock: The Healing Power of Electroconvulsive Therapy*

For about six months, I toiled away in my warehouse office, doing my best to convert the founders' content into trainable material, making two attempts at pilots, both of which bombed, I did my best to create a curriculum, delivered two pilot programs, both of which bombed, a result I hold myself partially responsible for. Perhaps the potential was there for a valuable training program and I missed seeing it—a very real possibility. I've always worked in a team environment, gaining valuable insights for those with different perspectives. Perhaps I would have had a better chance to create successful training with the benefit of a collaborative environment—colleagues with whom ideas could be bounced off, gaining the value of a synergistic approach. Yet this was the job I'd signed up for, fully aware I'd have one person to rely one—myself. Yes, the conditions were less than ideal, and I fully accept my role in the failed endeavor.

The View from Under My Desk

The end of this sad experience was, for the first time ever, I was fired. The nature of the depressive mind is to default to seeing the worst in oneself, which is how I internalized this ignominious ending.

To make matters worse, I was informed that my services would no longer be needed on my wife's birthday. The mood in my house that day was beyond somber. Depression was hitting hard. I'd just been through two failed jobs, had no prospects, and was aging—and no depression treatments were working. I'd abandoned vagus nerve stimulation, and was wearing a magnet, held in place on my chest with adhesive tape to turn off the pulse generator, which created a choking sensation every 30 seconds. I'd located another psychiatrist primarily for anti-anxiety drugs, since I'd tried every antidepressant and had no intention of trying more.

Adding to the Stigma

As my situation became more and more dire, I reflected upon the experience Kitty Dukakis had with ECT. I read that the procedure was the gold standard in depression treatments. The more I read, and the more I suffered, the more convinced I became that I wanted to undergo this stigma-laden treatment. This in spite of the fact that the medical community clearly stated in all of its descriptions that its mechanism of action was unknown. Speculation existed, but no research showed how putting the brain into a convulsive state, repeated several times, relieved suffering.

ECT comes with potential downsides and happens to be highly stigmatized—Thomas Eagleton, the 1972 Democratic Vice Presidential nominee, was shamed off the ticket by a national press hungry for dirt when it was discovered he'd undergone ECT. The stigma attached to the procedure was all the opposition needed to force the candidate out of the running.

There are different forms of ECT, some milder than the other. In unilateral ECT, one electrode is placed on the crown of the head and the other on the right temple. Unilateral ECT results in less short-term memory loss than its counterpart, bilateral ECT, but it is not as likely to reduce depressive symptoms. Bilateral ECT treatment involves placing the electrodes on both temples. This treatment may be associated with more acute memory side effects than right unilateral treatments. Bilateral ECT is indicated for severe mental illnesses including depression with psychosis, manic episodes of bipolar disorder, psychosis related to schizophrenia, and catatonia. After doing my research, I concluded that if I were to have ECT treatments, they'd be of the unilateral type, which had fewer side effects, including memory loss. This may have been a miscalculation on my part— perhaps the bilateral version would have given me the benefits Kitty Dukakis experienced.

The thoughts of having ECT performed at all were terrifying to me. At the time I was considering having it done, I was seeing a psychiatrist who was less than enthusiastic about its claims. In fact, there are various websites devoted to proclaiming its dangers. Images of Jack Nicholson undergoing a crude form of ECT in *One Flew Over the Cuckoo's Nest* are often cited to further stigmatize the treatment, striking fear into the hearts of those who might be considering it. But the pain of my depression was unrelenting. None of the psychotropic drugs I'd taken had helped, save for my experience with Effexor, which I'd tried many times in the ensuing years with no benefit, and Dukakis made a compelling case for the treatment.

So once again, I decided to pursue a treatment technique that, at a minimum, guaranteed short-term memory loss. And the logistics of getting to and from a hospital 50 miles from my home, with patients being strictly forbidden from driving following treatments, posed its own set of problems. I needed a total of twelve treatments. That meant that even by taking an early morning bus to the hospital, I'd need to arrange for twelve return trips, significantly inconveniencing those who would gather me up after the procedures and drive me home, a two-hour round trip. Fortunately, between family and friends, I found kind-hearted people to transport me home from the hospital.

The treatments began in mid-December 2008 and resumed following the holidays in January.

The first treatment was one of unspeakable physical pain. Apparently, the ECT psychiatrist had instructed the anesthesiologist to administer the dose of general anesthesia at too low a level. The goal is for the patient to be completely unconscious, unable to experience the effects of his brain being shocked into a seizure. Being heavily, though not completely sedated as I should have been, I experienced a level of discomfort that is impossible to describe. It was like being in a horror movie, but the horror was real. I was fully aware of what was going on, which was indescribable pain, but unable to communicate my extreme discomfort to the staff. Finally, summoning every ounce of will I possessed, I mumbled something that should have startled the two doctors, since I was supposed to be completely out. Fortunately, they figured out that I'd been given too low a dose, and immediately increased the level of anesthesia. The only effects from the next eleven treatments were mild headaches, which are to be expected, and nothing like the nightmarish event I'd undergone the first time around.

    So what was the result of all that time, effort, hope, money, and driving to receive the "gold standard" in depression treatment? Nothing. Nada. And what about side effects? A few months after that holiday break from the weekly ECT sessions, I came upon a photograph of Debbi, my grandchildren, and me, sledding down a hill near our home. I had absolutely no recollection of that event. Another failed attempt. I'd run out of options. I knew of no other treatments, however radical or mundane, to pursue. Having exhausted every treatment psychiatry had to offer, I would encounter my true rock bottom moment in the next few months.

Chapter 17: Hitting True Rock Bottom

"The question regarding addiction we should be asking isn't why the addiction, but why the pain."
Dr. Gabor Maté

I was at a stalemate. Shortly after my failed experiment with ECT, I'd obtained a script for sleeping meds, this for one that promised to get me asleep and keep me asleep, a drug called Lunesta, along with an anti-anxiety medication called Halcion. Once again, I developed a dependence on this drug. Not long after obtaining these pills, I made an impulsive trip to Boise, Idaho, a six-hour drive from my home, where I was to meet a friend about an idea I had. I went there to discuss a possible film project, a real long shot that consisted of a vague idea about ethics and leadership, with no idea where the financing would come from, and no idea how it would be distributed. I was really grasping at any idea that popped into my head, was on a trip and had run out of my meds. I hadn't thought about the consequences of depleting my supply of sleeping and anti-anxiety drugs. I had one Lunesta pill left to help me sleep, and no way to refill my prescription for either drug. So after running out of Lunesta that first night, I was desperate. By mid-afternoon, anxiety was kicking in and I had no means of relief. The only remedy that occurred to me was one I abhorred, which consisted of Tylenol PM, a combination pain reliever and sleep aid. I hated the way they made me feel in the morning and had vowed to never take them again after a previous unpleasant experience with them. But absent pharmaceuticals, they were the only alternative I could think of.

Hitting True Rock Bottom

With anxiety kicking in with a vengeance, I asked my friend to drive me to a drug store, where I purchased a bottle of this dreaded over-the-counter medication. He could tell that I was in bad shape and asked if these pills helped. I replied that they didn't but had no other options. I apologized for leaving before we'd had a chance to discuss the film idea, but knew I had to get to the PA for something stronger. The drive from Boise to Orem still haunts me. Every mile was excruciating. I met my wife just as she was getting ready to turn in and explained my predicament. For the thousandth time in our marriage, she said she was sorry to see me in such bad shape. Since I snore, keeping her from sleeping, I went to another bedroom for a completely sleep-free night. As soon as the doctor's office opened the next morning, I called and scheduled the PA's first appointment.

As we met, I confessed everything. I told him I'd just gone through a series of ECT treatments, which he had previously encouraged me to do, explaining they hadn't helped. I next told him of my earlier dependence on the narcotics he'd prescribed and had the audacity to ask him to give me a prescription for Oxycontin, which didn't produce nausea, one of the most potent and addictive of all the opiates, but clarified that this was a short term fix and that I wanted his help in weaning off them as I detoxed. I also asked for some sleep meds, along with some anti-anxiety pills, and to my surprise (and delight) he complied with all three requests.

But as soon as I'd procured the drugs, my good intentions went out the window. I immediately began exceeding the daily recommended dose of the Oxycontin and was on the fast track to dependence. I soon ran out. My short-term attempt at living a drug-free life had gone out the window as I quickly depleted my supply. I still possessed a small amount of Halcion, an anti-anxiety medication, but they were dwindling fast.

This was all taking place in late March, and my wife and daughter were getting ready to drive to St. George, a city in southern Utah where I'd made reservations for a family vacation over spring break. I was in such bad shape from withdrawing from three different drugs that I knew I'd be miserable, and miserable to be around, so I decided to stay behind and suffer by myself, hoping not to get in the way of everyone else's good times. But by Friday, my wife convinced me to drive down with my son. I was about to have a humiliating and embarrassing conversation enroute.

Fired by My Doctor

I'd been seeing a PA, or physician's assistant, for many years, never having met the doctor whose practice the PA worked for. Tragically, this doctor's son had just overdosed on heroin and died. I believe this accounted for what was about to happen to my status as a patient. Earlier that week, I'd emailed the PA, requesting some more anti-anxiety drugs. He'd replied that the doctor, who had to approve such requests, was getting jumpy, and that he wanted to speak to me. As my son and I began our four-hour drive to St. George, I received a call from the doctor. He informed me that he no longer wanted me as a patient. He'd been going through all his patient's files, identifying those who'd been receiving narcotics and other controlled substances, like anti-anxiety meds. With my son listening to the entire conversation, I tried to explain that I needed a refill of Halcion, and that without them, I would be in terrible shape and unable to sleep.

With no sensitivity to my plight (I was detoxing and coming down hard), and with the recent loss of his son, he had no sympathy for me and asked what I wanted from him, clearly wanting to get off the phone. A medical professional should have recognized the signs of detoxification, yet I could tell from his tone that he wanted to end the call as quickly as possible. I wanted to be reasonable, so I asked for a couple of days' worth of pills. He complied, but I hadn't asked for enough to adequately detox, and knew I was in for a hellish weekend. He concluded by saying that he was firing me as a patient, and that I was no longer welcome in his office. In view of his son's recent overdose, his actions were understandable, although not medically sound. This conversation was taking place within the closed confines of my car, with my son hearing every word. The minimal amount of Halcion I'd requested would not see me through the weekend, and as I went to the pharmacy in St. George to pick up my four pills of Halcion, I was dreading life and the hell I was about to experience.

    The Halcion were quickly consumed, and that Friday night I stole an Ambien my wife had in her purse for nights she couldn't sleep. The next day, I played golf with my two sons, but detox is a special form of hell, and I could barely swing a club. That night, I suffered immeasurably. I was completely unable to sleep. The next day, Sunday, I drove home in severe distress. I thought that the exhaustion from not having slept the previous night would allow me to at least find some relief in sleep. But it was not to be, and the next morning, with my friendly PA no longer a possible source of help, and after a desperate search, I found a pain clinic and was their first patient as they opened their doors.

    The simple act of filling out their intake papers was next to impossible, given the pain of detox and the lack of sleep during the past 48 hours. With my wife by my side, I was assigned a PA, who could only see a pathetic patient, showing no indication of a sense of urgency to alleviate my sad state. A doctor eventually appeared, who proceeded to give me a lecture on opiate and anxiety medication addiction. His dissertation on opiate agonists was filtered through the mind of someone needing help, which he was certainly in no hurry to dispense. I understood little of his scientific jargon. Unbelievably, I spent the entire day at a clinic with a mission to assist people with pain. Finally, as closing time neared, he wrote a prescription for Suboxone, a drug intended to alleviate withdrawal symptoms. As

I was in no condition to drive to the pharmacy, Debbi got the script filled, which I'm sure was a source of embarrassment for her, and by 6pm, after a full day spent in agony, I took a pill that temporarily ameliorated my distress.

The remainder of 2009 was a fog. I had been taking a lot of different drugs for a long time, and my mind wasn't what it had been when I wasn't pummeling it with pharmaceuticals. I was barely functional and had a hard time simply expressing myself. Work was out of the question in light of my impaired state and limited opportunities. So I took care of the yard and the pool, but I didn't have much of a life. True rock bottom had been reached.

It was August of that year when my mother passed at the age of 77 from an overdose of psychotropic medications. I had mixed emotions upon learning of her death. On the one hand, she was my mother, and I would never see her again. Yet her suffering was over, however her death had come. She'd once confided in me when I went to visit her during a stint in rehab that her father had deserted his family for another woman when she was twelve, leaving my grandmother and her four children to live in poverty. This news of my grandfather's negligence broke my heart, yet she never stopped loving him, and always looked forward with great eagerness to his infrequent visits to our house. Perhaps I'm not 100% accurate in my assessment that her mental illness was entirely biological. Perhaps some of her sadness derived from being abandoned by her father as a child.

The View from Under My Desk

Chapter 18: My $8/hour Gig

"Basically, I think you need two things to get by in this world: a sense of humor and the ability to laugh when your ego is destroyed."
Arlo Guthrie

During my heyday at Covey, I had one year when my compensation was over $400,000 in the early '90's and I was an owner worth $6 million—before the stock tanked. By now, I'd lost about 90% of my net worth, a substantial amount in a case of stock fraud, some to incompetent investment advisors who were losing my money as the stock market made significant gains and some to poor decisions on my part.

I desperately needed income, and just as importantly, I needed to rejoin the working world, performing some type of useful task. There is a ski rental shop about a mile from my house, conveniently located on the highway to Redford's Sundance Resort. Seeing no better prospect, one November day I ratcheted up my courage and drove into the parking lot of this ski shop to ask for a job. Feeling embarrassed at the thought, I turned my car around and vowed to call the owner, who I knew, rather than speak to him directly. Our relationship was based on infrequent encounters at Sundance when I was a big dog executive holding corporate retreats and he was the director of the ski school. So he'd only known me when I was a somebody, and who knew how he'd react to being asked for a job by a former Covey executive? Embarrassment and humiliation were my dominant emotions as I contemplated approaching the owner about a job most high school students could perform.

On the short drive back to my house, I argued with myself that the likelihood of securing a job in the ski shop would be higher in a face-to-face encounter than through a phone call. But how could I put myself through the shame of turning my car around and asking for a job, likely to pay minimum wage, putting ski boots on little kids?

Intuitively Practicing Radical Acceptance

Radical acceptance is a component of a type of therapy developed by Dr. Marsha Linehan. I didn't know it at the time, but my ability to turn my car around and head back to the ski shop was an instance of practicing radical acceptance. An article in the *New York Times* describes Linehan's early experiences with mental illness. *"She learned the central tragedy of severe mental illness the hard way, banging her head against the wall of a locked room. Marsha Linehan arrived at the Institute of Living on March 9, 1961, at age 17, and quickly became the sole occupant of the seclusion room on the unit known as Thompson Two, for the most severely ill patients. The staff saw no alternative: The girl attacked herself habitually, burning her wrists with <u>cigarettes</u>, slashing her arms, her legs, her midsection, using any sharp object she could get her hands on. The seclusion room, a small cell with a bed, a chair and a tiny, barred window, had no such weapon. Yet her urge to die only deepened. So*

The View from Under My Desk

she did the only thing that made any sense to her at the time: banged her head against the wall and, later, the floor. Hard." During the time she was locked down, she would later recall: *"I was in hell,"* she said. *"And I made a vow: when I get out, I'm going to come back and get others out of here."*

Linehan would recover and eventually earn her PhD in psychology, after which she developed her approach to treating suicidal patients, which she calls Dialectical Behavior Therapy. There are books on D.B.T., complete with worksheets for those seeking to apply its principles, and not being a clinician or having received training in D.B.T, I will not attempt to describe it or how it works. But I know it's a potent form of therapy from practicing one of its components on my own, as well as reflecting upon how I unknowingly followed its tenets in the ski shop scenario.

An introduction to radical acceptance can be found at: http://www.hselfhelp.com/html/radical_acceptance_part_1.html.

This is the only source of information on the topic from Linehan herself I've been able to find. My description of it is somewhat superficial, and I encourage anyone with an interest in learning more to go to the website.

Linehan uses the word *radical* to mean "absolute." "It's when you accept something from the depths of your soul. When you accept it in your mind, in your heart, and even in your body. It's total and complete." When you've radically accepted something, you're not fighting it. It's when you stop fighting reality. By turning the car around to go back to the ski shop, I was radically accepting my reality, which was that I was unemployed, needed to do something to get back into the workforce, battled depression on a daily basis, and work would be a partial remedy for that very depression that bedeviled me.

Radical acceptance involves three stages. First, we have to avoid denial and wholeheartedly accept our reality as it is. In Linehan's words, "What is the reality that you are denying? What are you not accepting for what it is?" When I first fled from the ski shop, I had been denying the reality I faced, which was a lengthy period of unemployment with no foreseeable options. By stopping the car and turning around, I accepted the reality I was facing.

Second, we must accept that the painful event or situation has a cause. Linehan explains that is the opposite of saying "why me." Saying that something "should be" is non-acceptance. There are things that cause things to be the way they are, even if the cause isn't clear to us. We have to believe that the universe is not out to get us, even when it feels that way. There were clearly causes for my lack of employment: my inability to cope with the stress of re-entering the workforce after a long hiatus during which skills had atrophied, the shakiness of my next employer and the resultant failure there, battles with depression, aging, and fallout from the decision to leave Covey with no intention of immediately rejoining the workforce. This ski shop incident occurred during the depths of The Great Recession, not a prime time for the unemployed to secure solid

The View from Under My Desk

jobs.

The final stage of radical acceptance is accepting that life can be worth living even with painful events in it. To go from unendurable agony to endurable pain, you have to believe that a meaningful, satisfying life can result. We realize there are positive things in our lives, even in the bad times, that make it worth fighting through our problems. This reminds me of the previous strategy of practicing gratitude. In spite of the hell I'd put her through, my wife still loved and supported me, as did my children. I lived in a nice neighborhood in a house that was paid for. My family was healthy and my children were thriving. Becoming more mindful of those things for which I'm grateful, when I remember to do so, has made the pain of depressive illness more endurable.

Finally, Linehan strongly advises the practice of radical acceptance every day. "This is not one of those things you're going to get perfect at," she says. "There's not going to be a day when you can say, 'Alright, I've got it; I can radically accept.'"

Turning My Car Around

It was with great effort I turned the car around and headed back to the shop. But simply pulling into the parking lot wasn't going to get me the job, and it was with still more intense effort that I opened the car door, walked into the shop, acknowledged the owner, and somewhat awkwardly asked for a job. Before he could answer, I wanted to give him an out, so I said something like, "Just give a call if you're interested" and started to leave the store.

To my surprise as I was exiting the shop, the owner called me back, and said, "Well, let's talk about it. Have you ever worked in a ski shop before?" "Yes!" I enthusiastically replied, not mentioning that it had been in the early '70s and that my skills might just be a bit rusty. To my shock and amazement, he offered me a job on the spot, not indicating what I'd be paid, just that I should show up the following Saturday for training.

The shop was tiny, with only two other workers, and I knew their customer base had to be small, so I wasn't expecting much in the way of compensation. But imagine my surprise, a former co-owner of a multi-million-dollar company, making almost a half million a year, when the boss informed me I'd be getting paid $8 an hour for my part-time, temporary gig putting ski boots on little kids and hauling their gear out to their parents' cars. Since the shop is in my neighborhood, it wasn't uncommon for people I knew to rent their skis there. A common question I'd get from customers who knew me was, "So, you're just helping out, right?" believing I was retired and was doing this to fill my empty hours. "No," I'd reply, "I'm working here" and I received more than a few puzzled looks from folks who'd known me in a different life. Business was usually slow, and I would often be sent home early, having worked a couple of hours.

From where I'd been at the height of my career, to this lowly status of ski shop worker, I

The View from Under My Desk

adapted remarkably well. I hustled to meet customer needs, did all sorts of odd jobs, and was shocked at how much I had to learn to be worthy of $8 an hour. Working there involved much more than simply showing up. I even had to pass an online test to qualify to mount boots to skis, which I passed with flying colors. This willingness to show up, work hard, learn new skills, admit to mistakes I'd make, receive feedback on my performance, and enthusiastically serve got me back in the game of work as I proved to myself that I could handle a dose of humility.

Looking back, it's easy to see how I might have shown an unwillingness to adapt to a new reality. Here I was, at the stage of life when most people are at their peak earning years and I was starting over at a job I'd done as a college kid at essentially minimum wage. I could have resisted learning the skills needed to actually be of value to the owner and his customers by telling myself I'd once worked in a shop and there was nothing more to know. I could have been fearful of exposing my ignorance to the boss and the two other employees who worked there, hiding the mistakes I was bound to make and seeking to appear competent and poised. I'll admit there were moments when I seriously questioned my sanity in thinking the ski shop was a desirable place of employment. I had to battle a sense of entitlement, that the world owed me more than this meager role of alternatively standing around battling boredom with my iPhone while waiting for the rare appearance of an actual customer during weekdays, to struggling to keep up with the frenetic pace of a busy Saturday morning. To my surprise, I found that I was capable of achieving new levels of humility.

    Unfortunately, the ski season at Sundance is short, ending around the first week in April, and my "lucrative" job in the ski shop was about to end. At least there was the next ski season to look forward to. I'd learned that life can indeed be worth living even with painful events in it, like being a lowly ski shop worker. And infinitely more valuable than the money I earned, the job had enabled me, albeit for too short a time, to rejoin the ranks of the employed. It taught me that I could learn new skills in a new environment with new co-workers, it taught me to admit to mistakes and actively listen to corrective feedback, and perhaps most importantly, it taught me to deal with the daily challenges I faced by exerting effort rather than believing my abilities to succeed in this bottom-of-the-rung job were fixed in stone.

Chapter 19: A New Beginning

"Although no one can go back and make a brand-new start, anyone can start from now and make a brand-new ending." ~ Carl Bard

Being unemployed once again in the spring of 2010 did not start well. On the Sunday morning during March Madness, I woke up with depression so overwhelming that I vowed to try anything—*anything* that might turn off this nightmarish existence. So I phoned my new family doctor, having yet to be fired by this one, and told him I was depressed. An earnest and seemingly genuinely concerned physician, he wanted to help, but his options were limited. I knew this going in.

So after writing a prescription for Prozac, a drug I'd tried more times than I cared to recall, he asked a fateful question, one that showed he knew something about depression. How was my sleep? I knew the answer I should have given—that my sleep was fine but thank you for asking. I also knew what would happen if I said otherwise: he'd write a prescription for Ambien, and as soon as I got my hands on the little white pills, I'd go on a binge. Taking Ambien during the day simply dulls the depression temporarily and creates significant cognitive impairment. Conversations held just minutes ago are forgotten, for instance. So why take Ambien except for sleep? Because they temporarily turn down the depression for a less painful, but certainly not pleasant experience.

Depression and the possibility of receiving pharmaceuticals to temporarily blunt its pain do terrible things to one's sense of honesty. The doctor proceeded to write a prescription for twenty days' worth of Ambien. They were gone in four, leaving me in horrific detox on day five. As I've described, detox involves practically unbearable anxiety, combined with insomnia. Now I really did have a sleep problem. I promised myself to avoid the insidious Ambien forever. It's been several years since that hellish week, and I've kept my promise.

The Silver-Haired CEO Returns

Around this time, I received a message on Facebook from Bob, the former CEO of The Seven Habits organization, the one who'd been terminated. Bob wanted to talk, so I called him. He'd been consulting with a small training firm in Provo, a business no more than five minutes from my house that I'd never heard of, flying in from his home in San Diego to offer his expertise. He believed this business, a training company that taught school teachers how to work with at-risk youth, urgently needed my expertise. I agreed to a meeting with Hans, the CEO, which turned into another meeting, and then spent the better part of a day with the company's founder, Christian Moore. He was a hyperkinetic fellow who'd earned a master's degree in social work, along with his credential as a licensed clinical social worker, all in spite of having severe learning disabilities and a highly dysfunctional upbringing. These are remarkable accomplishments

The View from Under My Desk

when you consider that less than one-half of 1% of people with learning disabilities achieve a graduate degree.

He proceeded to unleash his vision of his life's mission, which turned out to be writing a book for an adult audience and creating a training curriculum to teach the world resilience. Based on my work at Covey in creating the *Seven Habits* curriculum, Bob had convinced him I was absolutely necessary to bring his dreams to fruition. Christian can talk non-stop for hours on end, and as a highly enthusiastic professional speaker, with a personal audience of me, he went on for six hours without letting up. I didn't mention that I was used to working for stretches of only two hours at the ski shop before it was time for a break. Fortunately, there were some power bars and warm sodas in his office, which I gratefully devoured as I was a captive audience to this bundle of boundless energy, and lunch didn't seem to be imminent. Moore brought out a thick binder, filled with hundreds of pages of handwritten notes. These were his ideas that would change the world to a more resilient place, handwritten because his learning disabilities prevented him from understanding how to use a PC.

During brief interludes from this marathon verbal dump, I managed to share a few thoughts about how his concepts could be written and packaged. He must have been impressed, because the next day, I found myself once again hearing how resilience was desperately needed by society, how his own resilience had enabled him to overcome impossible odds, and how he desperately needed me

Depression and the possibility of receiving pharmaceuticals to temporarily blunt its pain do terrible things to one's sense of honesty. The doctor proceeded to write a prescription for twenty days' worth of Ambien. They were gone in four, leaving me in horrific detox on day five. As I've described, detox involves practically unbearable anxiety, combined with insomnia. Now I really did have a sleep problem. I promised myself to avoid the insidious Ambien forever. It's been several years since that hellish week, and I've kept my promise.

The Silver-Haired CEO Returns

Around this time, I received a message on Facebook from Bob, the former CEO of The Seven Habits organization, the one who'd been terminated. Bob wanted to talk, so I called him. He'd been consulting with a small training firm in Provo, a business no more than five minutes from my house that I'd never heard of, flying in from his home in San Diego to offer his expertise. He believed this business, a training company that taught school teachers how to work with at-risk youth, urgently needed my expertise. I agreed to a meeting with Hans, the CEO, which turned into another meeting, and then spent the better part of a day with the company's founder, Christian Moore. He was a hyperkinetic fellow who'd earned a master's degree in social work, along with his credential as a licensed clinical social worker, all in spite of having severe learning disabilities and a highly dysfunctional upbringing. These are remarkable accomplishments

The View from Under My Desk

when you consider that less than one-half of 1% of people with learning disabilities achieve a graduate degree.

He proceeded to unleash his vision of his life's mission, which turned out to be writing a book for an adult audience and creating a training curriculum to teach the world resilience. Based on my work at Covey in creating the *Seven Habits* curriculum, Bob had convinced him I was absolutely necessary to bring his dreams to fruition. Christian can talk non-stop for hours on end, and as a highly enthusiastic professional speaker, with a personal audience of me, he went on for six hours without letting up. I didn't mention that I was used to working for stretches of only two hours at the ski shop before it was time for a break. Fortunately, there were some power bars and warm sodas in his office, which I gratefully devoured as I was a captive audience to this bundle of boundless energy, and lunch didn't seem to be imminent. Moore brought out a thick binder, filled with hundreds of pages of handwritten notes. These were his ideas that would change the world to a more resilient place, handwritten because his learning disabilities prevented him from understanding how to use a PC.

During brief interludes from this marathon verbal dump, I managed to share a few thoughts about how his concepts could be written and packaged. He must have been impressed, because the next day, I found myself once again hearing how resilience was desperately needed by society, how his own resilience had enabled him to overcome impossible odds, and how he desperately needed me to help him bring this message to the masses. This man did not appear to be willing to take no for an answer, and he powered me through another six-hour session. There was no discussion of money, but that could wait.

Having just come off an $8/hour part-time seasonal job, and having no other job leads, I was intrigued. It was April 2010, and as it turned out through a series of unlikely circumstances, Christian was set to give a speech to a group of Walmart managers in Las Vegas during the week my family would be there for spring break. Both Bob and Christian enthusiastically expressed their desire that I attend, so with no expectations other than to keep the job discussions alive, I showed up at the Hard Rock Hotel to hear Christian give his first and only speech to a corporate audience.

Moore's standard keynote address is intended to motivate decision-makers in school settings to purchase his program, which is then taught to teachers as a means of reaching troubled youth. He'd been delivering this same message for years, and it was the only speech he had. How was he going to excite a group of grizzled Walmart managers with a speech designed for educators?

The beginning of his keynote involves telling his personal story, a compelling tale of growing up with severe learning disabilities and being mentored by an African-American woman he affectionately calls Mama Jackson. This woman would equip him with the social-emotional tools he'd need to navigate a rough home life, where he had no rules, as evidenced by his role as a drug mule at the age of seven for a group of teenagers.

The Walmart audience was mesmerized. The speech ended in a standing ovation. There was something here, I thought, as the attendees gathered around Christian. I'd just gotten my first glimpse at the talent that lay behind his relentless pursuit of a dream to deliver a book that would enable its readers to attain greater abilities to face life's inevitable adversities with a more resilient mindset.

After I returned home, Christian called. I was in my current home away from home, the local public library. I'd set up shop in a quiet corner with my MacBook Pro as I searched the Internet for jobs. Not wanting to disturb the other patrons, I made a quick exit into an empty space to take the call. It didn't go exactly as I had envisioned. I believe Christian was operating with the assumption that I was wealthy, in light of my Covey experience, and was simply searching for a way to fill time by helping him save the world through his gospel of resilience. He began the call by explaining that his company was small, and that money was tight. This was his way of working up to the punch line: he definitely wanted me to partner with him on his book but couldn't pay me.

At that point in the conversation, I lost it. How the hell did he think I would expend my efforts for free? And even if I did agree to his ridiculous proposal, why would he think that he was getting any value if he wasn't willing to reciprocate with some level of compensation? I was furious, having spent significant time in several interviews as well as the Las Vegas event. Undeterred, he countered that his organization had other wealthy, non-paid consultants who believed in its mission, and were only too happy to help advance the cause. I heatedly told him we had nothing more to discuss. He ended by saying he'd like to revisit an arrangement sometime in the late fall, and that was that. I didn't expect to hear from him again. Here was yet another failed job attempt which had seemed promising, only to evaporate because I was expected to work for free.

  So the summer dragged on, as I applied for any type of work that looked remotely promising. In light of my ski shop wage, I was willing to work at just about any job. I made numerous revisions of my resume, removing key roles I'd had in the past, such as VP at Covey, in an effort to dumb things down and communicate I was just an average guy, looking for an average job. Still nothing happened. Hope is hard to generate when every attempt at finding a job turns into futility. As the Great Recession dragged on, I'd read of accounts of people my age, unable to find work, taking their lives. This escape route seemed more and more appealing.

  Summer turned to fall, and out of the blue, Christian called once again. He and Hans, the CEO, had committed to writing the resilience book, and they wanted to know if I could attend a meeting in early January 2011. It was to be a kick-off meeting, a get-to-know you affair, and an effort to identify the project's objectives. Having no other possibilities, I agreed to attend, based on an hourly rate I told them I'd require. To my surprise, they agreed, and a date was set.

The View from Under My Desk

The Resilience Breakthrough

    The essence of the meeting was to set in motion the writing of a book about resilience. Christian wanted to do more than simply add to the thousands of books published each week. He wanted to make an impact and believed he had the content to do so. Moreover, he wanted the book to form the basis of his keynote speech on the topic, as well as the intellectual property for the training program that would emerge. In the beginning, the process consisted of Christian and me setting up shop in an empty classroom in the building where his company is housed and engaging in high energy exchanges of what resilience means, how it's developed, and listening to him tell one story after another as I recorded these sessions and sent them to a transcriber. We were an odd couple—this dynamo of boundless enthusiasm matched with my oftentimes flagging energy levels.

    It was not uncommon for Christian to return from a speaking trip and recount an incident from his travels. Many of these stories centered around conversations he'd have with seatmates in first class, as he was often upgraded due to his status as a two-million-mile flyer. I began to see these stories as material not only for the book, but also for presentations to audiences in speeches and training. As our meetings continued, I saw opportunities to validate Christian's ideas from the academic world. He wanted more than just another self-help book based on his thinking alone.

Rational Emotive Behavior Therapy—Again

After about three months of this process, I found myself in a meeting with Christian and Hans, the CEO. Not knowing the CEO well, as all my focus had been on Christian, I thought it might be useful to share with Hans the process I was using to mine as much valuable information from Christian as possible, explaining the interviewing process and how I got Moore to download stories, insights, and other experiences that would eventually constitute the book. There was one of those motivational posters hanging in the room, featuring the image of a dolphin along with an inspirational quote. Upon hearing of my role in generating the book's content, the CEO looked over at the poster and said, "You'd get the same results if you just sat Christian down and had him talk to the dolphin." I know what you're thinking—that this comment sent me spiraling into a fit of self-loathing, as my value had just been equated to that of a dolphin on a poster. However, I responded rationally and calmly, explaining that the process involved much more than sitting Christian in front of a recording device—if there was a time to be defensive, this was it—yet I managed my emotions quite handily.

I essentially followed the ABCDE model in responding to Hans. The activating event, or adversity, could have easily been interpreted as a demeaning comment. I responded by calmly re-explaining the value I was bringing to the project and did not descend into a pessimistic explanatory style. Christian indigently rose to my defense, clarifying that I was working feverishly to extract and organize information, and that the dolphin comparison was off base. It's hard having your worth equated to that of a fish, even one as smart as a dolphin. Yet I emerged unscathed and we plodded ahead.

It was only through the sheer force of will that I didn't allow depression to limit the number of hours each day I could work. There were some marathon sessions with Christian, followed by all the rest of the process I've described. I'd drive home and collapse. Christian worked me to the point of exhaustion, but it was a satisfying exhaustion.

Toward the end of the first year of the book project, I once again began having difficulty sleeping, and I was given a script for temazepam. Any drug ending in -pam is in the benzodiazepine class and all are potentially addictive. I believe Xanax has the most potential for abuse, and, for the most part, I have managed to stay away from them. But I would eventually become dependent on temazepam, which would land me in the emergency room.

Shooting Up a Club Drug

In February of that next year, Debbi casually mentioned that a co-worker's husband suffered from debilitating depression and had somehow found a psychiatrist in Salt Lake City who was experimenting with a new and somewhat controversial treatment using ketamine, otherwise known as Special K among club goers. Ketamine has been referred to as a date rape drug, as it puts its user into a weak, confused, and easily manipulated state. It's also used as an animal anesthetic. I had read reports in the news that some people with intractable depression had experienced almost instant relief from their symptoms on this drug and I had yearned for the opportunity to try it. My wife further explained that this man would be unable to afford the treatments, since they weren't covered by insurance. Neither were they covered by my wife's insurance, but I wasn't going to let a few hundred dollars, which was unfortunately significant because of the monetary losses we'd incurred, deter me from a potentially miraculous cure. Upon hearing of the possibility of ketamine treatments, I became almost frantic to learn more. What was her co-worker's name? Could I call and speak to her husband? Would he be willing to give me the name of the psychiatrist? Would I be able to make an appointment?

    The answers to my questions were all yes, and I made the earliest possible appointment. After meeting me and talking about my history with depression, the psychiatrist ushered me into a room that he'd prepared for ketamine injections. He had his nurse insert a needle into a vein in my arm, and then informed me of the process he'd follow. He explained that ketamine could cause hallucinations, but that the dose he was about to administer was low enough that I wasn't likely to trip out, as they said in the '60s. He then turned the lights down low in an effort to create a peaceful environment for the trip I was about to take, asked me to lie back on the table, and administered the drug. The experience wasn't unpleasant, in fact it was all quite relaxing, but as the drug wore off and he led me to the waiting room, I felt no anti-depressant effect.

Not losing faith, I would make two more attempts to allow ketamine to work its magic, at increasingly higher doses, yet I experienced no benefits. At the time, I was unaware that ketamine can be taken orally in capsule form, which I've since tried, experiencing some relief. The downside is that the effects are very short lived, and while under its influence, I'm unable to carry out normal daily functions. On more than one occasion while in a "K hole" my wife has called. She's been quick to point out that my speech was slurred and asked what drug I was on. The one advantage of ketamine in a capsule is that they've helped me through some particularly unpleasant events. But ketamine didn't work its wonders on my depression, and I've since stopped taking them.

On March 12, 2012, a Monday, I was about to experience yet another descent into the pain of detox. Christian, Kristin, our ghostwriter, and I spent the morning in an intense session and had taken a break for lunch. Both had appointments following our meal together, so after dropping them off back at the office, and in extreme distress, I drove myself to the emergency room due to the severe anxiety I was suffering, having run out of temazepam. Once again, I'd slipped into the habit of using sleep aids as anti-anxiety drugs during the days, and I was in extreme discomfort as the drug worked its way out of my body. As detoxification set in, my heart rate went crazy. The previous Saturday evening, I had walked to the local pharmacy in an effort to expend the pent-up energy I felt from the anxiety of withdrawing from this drug and took my blood pressure. The top number was over 160, putting me at risk for a stroke. After three brutal hours in the waiting area at the hospital, I was finally taken to a room in the ER. No one showed up. The anxiety was so severe I began doing pushups in an unsuccessful attempt to quell my distress. After another hour of torture, a kind social worker appeared and informed me that the doctors in the ER wouldn't treat me for withdrawal, and that I should contact my family doctor. On the surface, this sounded like a great plan, except it was now past closing time, and I wasn't about to admit to my friendly family doctor that I'd been abusing the drugs he'd prescribed—I'd already been fired by my previous doctor and didn't want a repeat of that humiliating experience.

    In my case, building up a tolerance to a particular drug takes no time, but the process of re-setting my body and getting off it is interminable. It took months before I wasn't wracked with anxiety. Performing my job while working through this daily battle was accomplished solely on will power. I later learned, much to my dismay, that the ketamine-prescribing psychiatrist would have helped me detox with a milder anti-anxiety drug.

    Remember the quote, April is the cruelest month? That spring, as all springs, was harsh. In May, I attended the funeral of an uncle I hadn't been close to and found myself in such disarray emotionally that I didn't know how I could go on, even though I had a good job for the first time in years, and we were making solid progress on the book. And then it hit me: why hadn't I gone back to the ketamine prescribing psychiatrist and sought his help, albeit with the knowledge that ketamine was not for me? So with nothing to lose other than the doctor's fee, I threw myself at his mercy. I explained that many years prior I'd self-medicated with opiates. To my surprise, he handed me a script for Percocet, and I looked forward with great anticipation to finally getting some relief. What I would soon relearn was that in the intervening years, my body had somehow changed, and the pleasant high that opiates once produced now resulted in a nasty and unbearable case of nausea. Undeterred, I made another appointment, and explained my experience with Suboxone, which had the same intolerable effect.

Finding the Miracle Drug—Or So it Seemed

All this was taking place during the summer, and by early fall, the psychiatrist seemed to strike gold. Listening to my descriptions of extreme fatigue, he recommended Adderall, a stimulant much abused by high school and college students to enable them to pull all night study sessions, and increasingly by employees looking for a way to stay focused and work longer hours in their attempts to enhance job performance. Its primary use is to treat ADHD, which I didn't have, but his thinking was that its stimulant effects might be helpful. And they were. For several weeks, I thought I'd found nirvana.

I had energy. I was focused. And most importantly, I'd given depression the slip, at least temporarily.

But the anti-depressant benefits of Adderall came with some costs in the form of side effects that couldn't be ignored. Its stimulating effects made sleep impossible. At about this time, the pharmaceutical reps for a new drug called Saphris had been dumping boatloads of free samples on my psychiatrist friend, which he freely gave me to save the cost of this outrageously expensive drug, used to treat psychosis (which, fortunately, I don't have). Saphris has a sedating effect and is the only drug I've found that can overcome the stimulation Adderall produces, allowing me to sleep. And as is the case with almost all drugs, this one had its own side effects, the worst being appetite increase and the resultant weight gain.

In addition, Adderall raises blood pressure, so I was prescribed yet another med to prevent me from having a stroke. So one drug led to another drug and so on. It's been over three years since that first dose of Adderall. Drugs have become an integral part of my life. And they're expensive and come with side effects. I found that I could save money on the obscene price of Saphris by cutting them in half. In addition, Adderall tends to increase anxiety, so I've been taking a small dose of Klonopin, known generically as clonazapam. Here was yet another pharmaceutical with side effects so dangerous that abruptly stopping it can cause seizures and death. Stevie Nicks of Fleetwood Mac fame had this to say: *"In comparison to the eight years I spent on Klonopin, the cocaine and brandy*

The View from Under My Desk

wins hands down. If you are ever in a drugstore and they put you on Klonopin, run out of there screaming." In my case, I take a small dose, one milligram/day, and sometimes don't take any. That's a lot of pharmaceuticals, but the combination has enabled me to get through the day and write this book.

I've learned an important lesson about pharmaceuticals: always do your research on a drug's side effects, along with what to expect when stopping, before deciding to use them. I've found over and over again that doctors, at least in my experience, have never discussed side-effects with me when prescribing a new medication. With the opiate epidemic raging, and the increased awareness this plague has created, perhaps physicians are doing a better job of informing their patients about what to expect when prescribing a new drug; my intention is to encourage a buyer-beware attitude by taking responsibility to gain a more complete picture of what one is about to ingest.

As valuable a drug as Adderall has proven for me, it's clearly not a cure-all. The depression I experience is ever present, sometimes more intense and sometimes less so. There are still times when I leave work and end up at home on the couch, trying to find relief by simply lying down. It's during these episodes that I'll feel desperate for relief, summon all the will power I possess by rising from the couch, mix a drink of caffeinated Crystal Light, and reach for a pill. Then I'm off to work again, hoping the effect lasts long enough for me to function like a normal person with a normal mood state.

Ironically, Adderall, gives me the energy to fight through the day, but leaves me depleted by day's end from over stimulating my body. I think of the amount of expendable energy like the water in a sponge soaked in water. By nighttime, the sponge is wrung out, with nothing left to give. I try to get through fatigue-based evenings by distracting myself with John Grisham novels and Netflix, but by 9:30 pm, a time most people are still active and moving about, I'm looking forward with great anticipation to going to bed. I rarely make it to 10pm, with my wife in the TV room, either reading or watching one of her favorite shows. If I've had a particularly lousy day, it's not uncommon for me to turn in at 9. And I want to be crystal clear on this point I made earlier about Adderall: I am not recommending it to address anyone's depression. Each person must find his or her own course of treatment. Adderall is a potentially addictive drug and must be used with great caution. I've already mentioned some of its side effects. Perhaps most dangerous of all is its tendency to create dependence over time, leading to worsening depression if it's not taken on a regular basis, and, as with any drug with the potential to be abused, greater amounts of this stimulant must be taken to achieve the desired effect, with addiction a possible outcome. At one of our frequent meetings, Christian made a comment that has stuck with me. I'd revealed some, but not all, of my financial and employment setbacks throughout our many sessions. He said that he'd been glad I'd gone through those unhappy experiences because if he was going to write a book about resilience, he didn't want to write it with someone who'd sailed unscathed through life. He saw the chaos of my life as a positive, enabling me to possess a greater sensitivity to those souls he hoped to reach with his book. Whether the adversities I'd endured were beneficial to writing the book is an open question, but it was nice to know he saw them as more than simply personal failings. To this day, I've never spoken with him about my battles with depression, but I think he's savvy enough to know it when he sees it. He saw what others would surly have seen as anathema in considering a new hire. For him, it as all positive. It's a tribute to my good fortune and mostly to his insight into knowing exactly the type of person who could add value, that made me feel the universe had smiled upon me. His absolute confidence that I was a partner and an employee who would be bringing a significant *advantage* by being depressed does wonders to restoring one's confidence.

    During our frequent meetings to discuss the content of the book, Christian and I would often go to lunch. He would look around the restaurant and size up the clientele. He'd then pick out a particular customer, oftentimes a well-dressed, attractive, and seemingly successful person, and ask me if I thought that person would read our book. He already knew the answer to his question, but wanted to hear my view. With the person in mind he'd identified, I replied that no, I didn't think that particular individual would see him or herself needing instruction in how to be more resilient. The real question Moore was asking was, "Is there a market for this book we're writing?"

    When he'd first thought of writing his book, he had in mind the person who he wanted to help: an inmate on death row, with thoughts of hanging himself. The patrons in the sometimes upscale restaurants Christian favored didn't fit that profile, yet his opinion that everyone, at some point in their lives, experiences extreme adversity, kept the fire alive. The world needed resilience, and he was about to bring it to them. How we would get the book published and made available to its target market wasn't on our minds at that point. The focus was on Christian's ideas for increasing resilience. The publishing and distribution would take care of themselves if we created a compelling read.

    It was now late 2012, and the book was nearing completion, although it hadn't seen the scrutiny of a professional editor. The process I'd set in place seemed to be producing a worthwhile document. A friend had just self-published a book and in his investigation of the publishing world, came across a hybrid-type publisher, nationally recognized, that produced the book for a fee and allowed the author to sell his or her own books and collect 100% of the revenues. I wrote and submitted a lengthy proposal that we hoped would be persuasive since we'd been told they were highly selective in the manuscripts they accepted for publication. And then we waited.

    Finally the call came: the publisher had thoroughly reviewed our book and had accepted it for publication.

The View from Under My Desk

Pawn Shops Enter the Picture

During this time, my garage was broken into and my golf clubs were stolen. Eventually the police officer assigned to my case called to inform me that the clubs had been located in three separate pawn shops in Salt Lake City, and that the name of the person who had pawned them was my next-door neighbor, who also happened to be my son in law. I was asked if I wanted to press charges. This was my daughter's husband, the father of four of my grandchildren. I hesitated before answering that no, I'd prefer to just have the clubs returned to me.

In my naiveté, another thing I didn't understand about pawnshops is that they're sources of money for drug addicts. When I confronted my son in law with the facts, he fabricated a story about how he'd run into some folks who were down on their luck and had invited them to his house, and that it was they who'd done the deed. This of course, made no sense since the pawnshop had given his name as the seller. Eventually my daughter would divorce this fine fellow, and when it came time to sell their house, the inspection turned up signs of significant methamphetamine use, which he tried to blame on a neighbor. The pain my daughter and her four children have endured through the ugliness of the divorce has caused a sequence of unending drama and my depression worsened as I witnessed the damage her ex-husband had on my daughter and her children. I try to manage my emotions by reminding myself that 50% of marriages end in divorce, many in acrimonious ways. Sometimes this helps, sometimes it doesn't. And when I remember to do so, I put radical acceptance into play—just not often enough.

The View from Under My Desk

Chapter 20: How to Avoid Becoming an A-hole Boss and What to do to Survive One

During a lunch meeting with a recruiter who was sizing me up for a position he was seeking to fill, I wanted to be fully transparent, and did something that most would consider an act of job-hunting suicide. I knew this individual from working with him at a previous company, trusted him, and went on to disclose that I battled depression, something I thought he should know.

I have no doubt there are few, if any, instances of a recruit revealing this kind of information in a setting where the norm is to show the person holding their fate in his or her hands nothing but their best and brightest characteristics. I was fully aware of risk I was taking in sharing that the person he was seated across the table from suffered a mental illness. My revelation left him unfazed. He said that, while he wasn't highly familiar with depression, the fact that his wife suffered from a somewhat severe anxiety disorder, had given him a sense of what I was attempting to communicate. He concluded our meeting by telling me he'd communicate his thoughts from our discussion with the hiring manager, and that he was confident I was the right person for the job.

What followed is my absolute best example of one of the most important goals I've had in writing this book. My recruiter friend did, in fact, report my disclosure of dealing with depression to the manager. The manager's response? *"What's depression?"* So what's this supremely important point I want to make? That if you are now, or someday will be, in a leadership role, you *will* be supervising employees struggling with depression.

I want this chapter to be beneficial not only for leaders, but to individual contributors, the folks tasked with actually getting things done in their organizations. So here's what's coming: some hard-won lessons from my career I want to share with leaders for managing depressives as well as those without mental health challenges, along with ways employees can better navigate their job circumstances when confronted with managers that almost everyone encounters at some point—those in leadership positions who, maliciously or not, create toxic environments. I hope that's enough encouragement for you to read on.

Know Your Role, Avoid Playing Therapist and Facilitate Getting Help For Those in Need

As a leader, your job is to create the conditions for the people reporting to you to thrive, to tap into their best selves, to draw out potential talents they may not have even been aware of. You are not trained to diagnose mental illness. Having made that point, you're still a fellow human traveler, and have experienced your own share of life's inevitable setbacks. Some leaders are more attuned to the emotional states of their people than others. It might be tempting to leap to the conclusion that a particular person is suffering depression or anxiety. The reality is you just can't be sure—again, you're not a trained therapist. Someone might just be having a tough time on the home front and will return to their normal self in time. With that said, there *are* signs of depression at work that can be hard to miss, especially if they persist. These include:

- Difficulty concentrating, remembering or making decisions
- A change in performance and on-the-job behaviors, such as decreased or inconsistent productivity
- Absenteeism, tardiness or frequent absence from workstation
- Increased errors and diminished work quality
- Procrastination and missed deadlines
- Withdrawal from co-workers
- Overly sensitive or emotional reactions
- Decreased interest in work
- Slow movement and actions

If you've noticed several of these, you should have a conversation with the employee, avoiding giving them a diagnosis, and sticking to what you've observed. Compassion is essential in such as discussion, avoiding any hint of judgment or displeasure. If you sense their discomfort discussing these issues with you, refer them to HR or your Employee Assistance Program is one exists in your organization.

Brad Anderson

Comorbidity—A Special Kind of Hell

Comorbidity is the simultaneous presence of two chronic diseases or conditions in a patient. For our purposes, it's the co-occurrence of depression and anxiety. It goes without saying but I'll say it anyway: depression alone, as I've tried to illustrate, is indescribably horrific. Now consider adding anxiety into the mix. Contemplate this from Andrew Solomon: *"If you told me that I'd have to be depressed for the next month, I would say, "As long I know it'll be over in November, I can do it." But if you said to me, "You have to have acute anxiety for the next month," I would rather slit my wrist than go through it. It was the feeling all the time like that feeling you have if you're walking and you slip or trip and the ground is rushing up at you, but instead of lasting half a second, the way that does, it lasted for six months. It's a sensation of being afraid all the time but not even knowing what it is that you're afraid of."*

So what does a leader do in the face of what must seem an impossible combination of conditions faced by one of his or her charges? I'll begin with what not to do. When I joined the training firm created by the four authors, I was hired for my training skills. What an irony that turned out to be. During those years Solomon tells us we can never get back, I'd lain on the floor, which isn't a great prescription to stay sharp in one's chosen field. In former days, as a young, confident corporate trainer, I'd stepped confidently in front of groups of General

The View from Under My Desk

Motors executives for example, and on numerous occasions, led corporate leadership trainings across the country and abroad, through three to five days of intense training. But this was a different time, I was different, and the technology was completely foreign to me. While other trainers nimbly navigated their laptops and Power Points, I stood back in awe, telling myself I could never do what I was seeing. The era of using a flip chart and VCR had long passed, and I was in catch-up mode.

After a couple of months trying to learn the ropes, I actually did approach my boss and ask if I could do a short executive briefing in San Francisco—scared out of my wits, but knowing I had to get going. He told me I wasn't ready, but neither was I told what to do to get ready. Whether anxiety is in the picture or not, it seems obvious to me that any employee about to undertake a new task requires coaching, feedback, perhaps more coaching, some praise if warranted, and then watch their confidence blossom.

So what lies below the surface, to then manifest into this mood state so intolerable Solomon talks about slitting his wrists to escape it? One factor is uncertainty, a lack of familiarity with a new task. Some seem to innately have that quality of knowing they can master most anything that comes their way. Describing anxiety to such an individual would result in glazed over eyelids. And then there are those that have the genetic and/or conditioning to become anxious at the slightest hint of uncertainty.

In addition to tackling the unknown, a sense of being overwhelmed is a definite trigger for me.

Of the many responsibilities leaders perform, determining to whom an assignment should go, and how much of a workload to require are among the most important. Use your knowledge of your people's strengths, weaknesses, levels of confidence, and any other information you've gleaned to determine who will require a bit more coaching, a bit more encouragement, a bit more checking in to find out if they're handling the workload as you expected. Put to use Kark Weick's discovery, discussed in Chapter 2, that research has shown that individuals, teams, and organizations that bite off too big a problem are setting themselves up for disappointment and frustration. Feeling overwhelmed can correlate with a sense of helplessness and giving up. As Weick puts it, *"Attaining even one small win can create the feeling that you are in control of something; this can reduce feelings of hopelessness and helplessness."* Help those who struggle figure out ways to break tasks into doable chunks and watch their projects progress as they achieve one small win after another.

And What of Workers Facing Toxic Environments?

Stanford's Bob Sutton wrote a blockbuster bestseller, with the somewhat cheeky but descriptive title, *The No Asshole Rule—Building a Civilized Workplace and Surviving One That Isn't.* I

The View from Under My Desk

underlined a passage in the book in which he refers to power poisoning (that phrase alone should serve as a serious warning to those entrusted with power): *"A huge body of research—hundreds of studies—shows that when people are put in positions of power, they start talking more, taking what they want for themselves, ignoring what other people say or want, ignoring how less powerful people react to their behavior, acting more rudely, and generally treating any situation or person as a means for satisfying their own needs—and that being put in positions of power blinds them to the fact that they are acting like jerks.* In a speech he gave at Stanford, Sutton distils the essence of his message on power. He notes that when a person is placed in a position of authority over others, the more powerful individual typically resorts to three behaviors: he or she pays less attention to the needs and wants of subordinates, he or she pays greater attention to their own needs and wants, and he or she behaves as if the rules don't apply to them. As I look back at my own managerial stints, I'm quite certain there were times Sutton's description of such bosses applied to me.

Sutton's book offers some guidance I wish I had known though out my career, as it came too late to do me any good. The subtitle is *Building a Civilized Workplace and Surviving One that Isn't*. He offers several suggestions to accomplish that last part about survival. One of my favorites is *Develop Indifference and Emotional Detachment*. I could have benefited from this numerous times in my career as I've invested too much of my sense of

In addition to tackling the unknown, a sense of being overwhelmed is a definite trigger for me.

Of the many responsibilities leaders perform, determining to whom an assignment should go, and how much of a workload to require are among the most important. Use your knowledge of your people's strengths, weaknesses, levels of confidence, and any other information you've gleaned to determine who will require a bit more coaching, a bit more encouragement, a bit more checking in to find out if they're handling the workload as you expected. Put to use Kark Weick's discovery, discussed in Chapter 2, that research has shown that individuals, teams, and organizations that bite off too big a problem are setting themselves up for disappointment and frustration. Feeling overwhelmed can correlate with a sense of helplessness and giving up. As Weick puts it, *"Attaining even one small win can create the feeling that you are in control of something; this can reduce feelings of hopelessness and helplessness."* Help those who struggle figure out ways to break tasks into doable chunks and watch their projects progress as they achieve one small win after another.

And What of Workers Facing Toxic Environments?

Stanford's Bob Sutton wrote a blockbuster bestseller, with the somewhat cheeky but descriptive title, *The No Asshole Rule—Building a Civilized Workplace and Surviving One That Isn't.* I

The View from Under My Desk

underlined a passage in the book in which he refers to power poisoning (that phrase alone should serve as a serious warning to those entrusted with power): *"A huge body of research—hundreds of studies—shows that when people are put in positions of power, they start talking more, taking what they want for themselves, ignoring what other people say or want, ignoring how less powerful people react to their behavior, acting more rudely, and generally treating any situation or person as a means for satisfying their own needs—and that being put in positions of power blinds them to the fact that they are acting like jerks.* In a speech he gave at Stanford, Sutton distils the essence of his message on power. He notes that when a person is placed in a position of authority over others, the more powerful individual typically resorts to three behaviors: he or she pays less attention to the needs and wants of subordinates, he or she pays greater attention to their own needs and wants, and he or she behaves as if the rules don't apply to them. As I look back at my own managerial stints, I'm quite certain there were times Sutton's description of such bosses applied to me.

Sutton's book offers some guidance I wish I had known though out my career, as it came too late to do me any good. The subtitle is *Building a Civilized Workplace and Surviving One that Isn't*. He offers several suggestions to accomplish that last part about survival. One of my favorites is *Develop Indifference and Emotional Detachment*. I could have benefited from this numerous times in my career as I've invested too much of my sense of worth into whatever job I was in, causing setbacks I've described to hit me particularly hard. Sutton cautions that when we're working in noxious environments that we not allow our self-worth to be dictated by how people treat us, and that investing all your effort and emotional energy into your workplace is a path to exploitation and self-destruction. *"Self-preservation sometimes requires the opposite response: learn to feel and practice indifference and emotional detachment...There are times when the best thing for your mental health is to not give a damn about your job, company, and especially, all those nasty people."* He then quotes Walt Whitman to buttress his point, *"Dismiss whatever insults your soul."* Had I practiced Sutton's strategy of developing indifference and emotional detachment with the young woman who attacked me in the volunteer role at the university, I might have avoided the disastrous decision to self-medicate my emotional pain with opiates.

It seems obvious, but I'll state it anyway. The relationship between one's direct boss and his or her employee can, and often does, play a major role in that employee's mental health. Learn to spot toxic bosses by using Sutton's two tests for what he refers to as Power Poisoning; and if you're a leader, ask yourself if you might have acceded to this all-too-common tendency: *"Test One: After talking to the alleged asshole, does the "target" feel oppressed, humiliated, de-energized, or belittled by the person? In particular, does the target feel worse about him or herself? Test Two: Does the alleged asshole aim his*

The View from Under My Desk

or her venom at people who are less powerful rather than at those people who are more powerful?" If you've determined that your boss meets these criteria, do your best to practice indifference and emotional detachment. And if you're fortunate enough to have other employment options, consider leaving the organization. He adds that when performance is going well for the executive, they especially become clueless and self-absorbed. Add these to your repertoire of tools in spotting difficult bosses.

Going all the way back to my college days, I once took a job in Idaho in a retail store. The products offered in my department were seasonal in nature, used during the warmer months of the year, and this was January in a cold state. I worked several shifts during which no one came by to even browse the items for sale. I hadn't been instructed to do this, but I often approached fellow employees in other departments, offering to help them out if needed. If a customer did enter my department, an employee at the front counter would alert me over the store's intercom. The employee I'd been helping would typically thank me for my efforts and I then hustled back, trying to find out how to best serve the customer's needs. Their response was almost always the same, "Just looking around." I often wondered how this department could be profitable, as sales were rare—but raising this question was far above my pay grade.

The store's hierarchy consisted of the general

manager, a couple of assistant GM's, department managers, and the worker bees such as myself. My department manager was rarely there when I was working, and occasionally another fellow department employee would show up.

One memorable Saturday morning began rather routinely. After vacuuming the carpet in my department, and with no customers in sight, I noticed that the next department to mine wasn't being staffed, saw this floor to be in need of my vacuuming skills, and proceeded to do the job. Right as I was finishing, I received one of those rare calls on my headset that a customer had entered my department. Not wanting to delay getting over to my area, I hurriedly rolled up the three, long extension cords connected to the vacuum, placed them on the vacuum's cord hook, and set the vacuum back behind the counter so that it wouldn't be in anyone's way, intending to return it to its proper location in the back room after finishing with my customer. Almost exactly as the customer departed, the general manager approached. Having never heard a positive word from him, such as a brief thank you for helping out other employees, I wondered what this was about. Not bothering to mention the extra-mile effort I'd gone to in vacuuming the department next door, he proceeded to berate me for not returning the vacuum to its proper location. My explanation of having seen a need (a dirty floor and no one to take care of it, the fact that the vacuum wasn't hindering anyone's path, that I'd been called to serve a customer, along with my intention to immediately

The View from Under My Desk

take care of the vacuum's storage) fell on deaf ears. Strike one.

Strike two was not long in coming. A little later in the day, a customer asked to inspect a product that was situated on a shelf, high up on the wall and requiring the use of a ladder to reach. After he'd inspected the product, he handed it back to me, and I climbed the ladder to put it in its place. As I did so, I jostled an adjoining shelf, and watched in horror as a product fell off that shelf, grazing the customer's sunglasses, and breaking them into two pieces. Beyond embarrassed and horrified, I offered my profuse apology, then grabbed a notepad to write down my name and the store's phone number—this was decades before cell phones. I handed the note to the customer, telling him to call me as soon as he'd identified the sunglasses to replace the one's I'd just broken, and that I would take care of paying for the replacement. Beyond apologizing and paying for the damage I'd caused, I had no other ideas for making amends.

How the general manager found out about the sunglasses incident I'll never know, but within minutes he showed up. Already stressed by what I'd done, I was about to experience even more. By this point in my relationship with this guy, I had no reason to expect anything but a dressing down—which I fully expected this time in light of my mistake. Expressing his displeasure with the damage I'd caused, which was clearly warranted, he went on to reprimand me for violating store policy. What store policy had I defied? I asked. In what appeared to be absolute frustration, I learned that my screw-up was that in any case of an employee causing damage to a customer's property, the policy was that the store was the responsible party, and that I'd been out of line in attempting to pay for the broken sunglasses. I'd never been informed of this policy, which I explained, along with telling him I'd done what I thought to be the correct thing in this situation. I clearly expected some form of censure, but his rebuke would have been much more tolerable had he recognized, that since I was unaware of the policy, offering to pay for the damages myself was at least a worthwhile gesture.

    I didn't have to wait for long, as the umpire was about to call strike three. An announcement went out that pizza had arrived in the break room, and for everyone to come grab a slice or two when they could. This was the rare day the department manager was at work, and seeing him behind the counter, and the standard absence of customers, I headed back for a welcome break. As I entered the room for my brief respite, I saw the GM and another front line worker, seated at a table with their pizza slices.

    Deciding to join them, and, and before even taking a bite, the general manager asked me a question, in a tone of derision that was validated by my fellow low-level colleague after the GM departed. He asked if I had informed the department manager that I was headed back to the break room.

The View from Under My Desk

Surprised by the question and doing my level best to maintain my composure in the face of this third critique in one day, I tried to explain the circumstances. Having rarely even been on the same shift with the department manager, I replied that I'd never heard of this expectation and that there were no customers to serve, naively expecting the GM to accept that as a reasonable explanation. I further suggested that I'd always been notified when a customer appeared, had immediately dropped whatever I was doing, and hastily made my way to the department. The GM was not impressed and continued to communicate his disgust. I didn't say what I believed to be so obvious as to not need saying, that if a customer had shown up, the department manager would have either dealt with him or her or called me for assistance. Having delivered his final blow, he finished his pizza and left.

    I've already mentioned that depressives are quick to internalize negative feedback as yet another source of evidence of their already low self-opinions. However, in this instance, my young, similarly college-aged and non-depressed fellow underling (at least that's how I saw him) weighed in. His exact words were, *"You shouldn't have to put up with that kind of crap."* As it turned out, this same employee had witnessed my experience with vacuum-gate. My thought following his observation/advice was, "Wow! I'm not so crazy after all! Someone else viewed the encounter exactly as I had."

Back to Dr. Sutton two tests for what he refers to as "power poisoning." *"Test One: After talking to the alleged asshole, does the "target" feel oppressed, humiliated, de-energized, or belittled by the person? In particular, does the target feel worse about him or herself?* My answers were yes, yes, and yes! My onlooker's comment was highly validating, although by this point I was in no need of validation—it was just nice to know a neutral observer saw precisely what I saw. Having spent my working days there in the complete absence of any form of recognition, praise, or even an occasional atta-boy, and the three particularly unpleasant performance critiques of that day, I was done, resigning in search of a healthier workplace.

As I later reflected about my experiences at the store, it occurred to me that every instance of negative feedback from the GM was characterized by a harsh tone, were doled out in the presence of others (a major mistake when criticizing someone), an absence of any acknowledgment of the positive things I'd done, and most importantly, that he had done nothing to set expectations for my on-the-job performance. Many years on, with the benefit of hindsight and Dr. Sutton's insights, it seemed clear that I had encountered a boss who'd succumbed to power poisoning.

Power is a reality in any organization. While not a perfect analogy, the framers of the United States Constitution recognized the dangers of concentrating power in the hands of one individual or one branch of government and incorporated the separation of powers, dividing the central government into three branches and creating a system of checks and balances. Used properly, power is essential for achieving the mission of a team, a department and an entire organization. Its abuse, an all too common phenomenon, is a leading contributor in producing toxic bosses and toxic workplaces. Sadly, it can become something of a narcotic, working it's bewitching qualities into a leader's style, without their awareness. Power's seductive lure, for those beguiled by this newly acquired status, results in a form of intoxication, along with a sense of entitlement (recall Sutton's description of the three things that can occur when someone acquires power, one being that the rules do not apply to them), slowly working its seductive influence, imparting a sense of supremacy. Former United States Secretary of State, Henry Kissinger, coined his famous phrase, *"Power is the ultimate aphrodisiac,* "ostensibly recognizing the enormous influence this attribute has upon those who fail to find ways to develop their own system of checks and balances.

As with any attempt to recover from an addiction, the first step in gaining the awareness that one has fallen victim to power poisoning, is gaining the awareness of the extent of the degree of control it exerts—how deeply insinuated it may have become in the fabric of one's leadership style. I've worked for many managers who knew how to use their power wisely, and others who were clueless, leaving a wake of destruction in their paths. My intention in this discussion of power is not to offer strategies for its proper handling, but perhaps more modestly, warn us all about the potential for corruption when wielding power, and to find our own system of checks and balances to avoid falling victim its potential deleterious consequences. Dr. Sutton is one of many excellent sources for learning more about power, and I highly recommend two of his books, *The No Asshole Rule—Building a Civilized Workplace and Surviving One That Isn't*, along with *Good Boss, Bad Boss—How to Be the Best...and Learn from the Worst*. His excellent blog, found at https://bobsutton.typepad.com/, is constantly being updated with the latest research and practical advice for becoming the best boss one can be.

The View from Under My Desk

Chapter 21: Current State of Affairs

My psychiatrist recently informed me he'd like me to start seeing a therapist, knowing that I've not been able to find one that's helped. He also pointed out that finding a good one wouldn't be easy. As my experience was to soon show, he got that right. Until I locate this elusive person, he's asked me to start using him as my therapist. As a person I enjoy seeing for discussions about psychiatric medications and life issues, we've gotten to know each other well over the past four years.

I'm hopeful that he can help on the talk therapy side of treatment. We've had a couple of sessions so far, which have seemed promising, but the need to discuss medications has made the therapy parts of our visits quite short. Soon after he made this request, I asked the head of therapy for an organization I'm familiar with if he had a recommendation. He gave me a name, and after calling and scheduling an appointment, showed up at the appointed hour. The experience would not go well. The therapist arrived 15 minutes late for starters. I get that people have other things to deal with, so I tried to let that one go. After asking me a few general questions, with 10 minutes remaining in the session, she asked for my credit card, announced that we were through and asked when I could return the following week. I pointed out two concerns: first, that the session had been well under 40 minutes in length, but more importantly, that she hadn't imparted any therapy. What tools was I to take away from our time together? I asked. She hurriedly printed out a two-page document on how to overcome OCD and told me it would be helpful in lessening my depression. Somewhat skeptically, I returned to my office and dutifully read the paper. It was completely irrelevant. I proceeded to text her that I wouldn't be returning based on the lack of value I received. Thus began my latest search for a therapist.

Failing to Find a Therapist

My next attempt would fare even worse. I don't think I'm a difficult client. I'm sincerely trying to find a skilled professional to help if help is to be had. At this stage of my life, I have nothing to hide—I'm an open book when it comes to revealing my struggles–which I assume is a quality therapists appreciate. I believe I've been respectful toward the therapists I have seen, have never lost my temper, and have answered all their questions as openly and honestly as possible. In other words, I want to cooperate fully in whatever healing process a therapist is pursuing. My first red flag came before I even met this fellow. Via email, he informed me that he would try to work me into his "busy schedule." I did my best to suspend judgment but thought it an odd way to introduce himself. I would soon learn that self-importance was one of his defining characteristics.

At our first meeting, I experienced him as competent but judgmental. I hung in there in spite of a noticeable lack of warmth and safety. When I answered his questions, he seemed to be going through the motions of listening, but not really. Prior to my third visit (see, I was really trying) I'd just read an article about Marsha Linehan of radical acceptance fame. I asked my new therapist what he thought of her approach. His response stunned me. "I would never use DBT (the name of her overall therapy approach)!" he exclaimed emphatically. I asked why. I was further stunned by his reply. "Because DBT was developed by a mentally ill person." I wanted to ask, "So, if I came up with an approach that proved to lessen someone's depression, you would dismiss it out of hand because I'm depressed?" But still wanting to keep things on an even keel, I kept my thoughts to myself.

    I mentioned my concerns with this therapist to my psychiatrist and he told me it didn't look like a good fit. But undaunted, I went a fourth time. At this session, he revealed the results of an extensive personality test he'd had me take. In a highly glib and hurried manner, he held up a sheet of paper with graphs and lines and peaks and valleys. I had no idea what this peak or that valley represented. I kept asking him to explain a particular term but I eventually realized he wasn't going to take the time to make sure I understood whatever implications the test held for me. I felt completely overwhelmed with data—not information, not knowledge—but data, data which gave me a feeling of drowning in a sea of vertical, horizontal and diagonal lines.

    To make matters worse, he delivered a boatload of psychological jargon in a highly imperious manner, seeming to take the role of God in pronouncing my pathology. There was no warmth, no inquiry as to my thoughts, no human touch of any kind. I asked him to call my psychiatrist, and was informed that he'd comply with my request, but that psychiatrists aren't trained to understand this test. Here are a couple of excerpts of what I got back from the doctor after the therapist and he spoke by phone: *"He'll send me the MMPI (the personality test I took). I understand it more than he realizes. And can help you understand it in a less derogatory way. I think this guy would be hard to work with. You need someone essentially sensitive, kind, safe. Possibly a woman. Please keep looking. Let's keep in touch."* The next day, I emailed the therapist that I wouldn't be returning.

Called to Coach

I'm 62 years old. I have lost most of my net worth, am in an unstable job situation, am looking at a highly uncertain future, and possess a mood disorder. Last summer, the company I worked for went through some bad financial times, and I was laid off for about four months, an unexpected and painful event. Being once again unemployed brought back the feelings of worthlessness I'd so often felt. After driving the company's new book to completion, along with creating a successful proposal to a respected publisher, the layoff was particularly stinging. I was eventually rehired at a reduced salary. But I am grateful for the work. It definitely beats my short-term stint at the ski shop.

But all is not bleak. I do have a job. My

The View from Under My Desk

family is, for the most part, thriving, with the exception of my daughter's devastating divorce, and she will hopefully recover from the trauma in her life. I own my house and cars and have no debt. I have friends and a caring and competent psychiatrist. I've been married for over 40 years, and my wife hasn't given up on me yet—depression has led to more than one divorce. Things could be worse. I have a lot to be thankful for.

    My wife and children know intimately the battles I wage and have the patience and love to accept my limitations without judgment and criticism. This doesn't mean they completely absolve me of my roles as father and husband—they still hold expectations I can fulfill, but their awareness does enable me to disappear into the bedroom on occasion without feeling I'm letting everyone down by not being part of family gatherings and activities. Sometimes, I can will myself to perform tasks in spite of the heaviness depression creates. Usually, it's because someone I care about needs me. Relationships motivate.

    For instance, during the past few summers, I've been the assistant coach on one of my granddaughter's baseball teams, a relatively easy job since someone else is responsible and I'm just there to help. With my nine-year old granddaughter's family in turmoil from her parent's divorce, I made a point early in the year to make sure she was signed up for girl's softball. I wanted her to have a fun and healthy activity that could briefly give her a break from the stress she's experienced from the divorce. But this year I've had to take on the head coaching role, because no one else would.

    As a young father, I coached my kids routinely. Now I find the need to dig deep to perform this role to support my granddaughter, which includes holding weekly practices with nine and ten-year-old girls, some of whom have never played before, along with coaching two games a week. Unlike her previous baseball teams when no scores or standings were kept, she has graduated into the realm of competition, with umpires, and scoreboards, and standings. I knew we were in trouble when one girl asked me where center field was located. Prior to the games, we'd hold short informal practices and try to give each girl a chance to bat, field and throw.

    The girls were excited for each upcoming game. The assistant coach was calm and rational. The parents appeared relaxed and at ease. Having coached years of youth sports with my own children, it would seem I'd take coaching my nine-year old granddaughter's team in stride. Such has not been the case. Following our first practice, which can only be described as a debacle, I looked at the upcoming season with dread and anxiety. Prior to the games I became anxious. To help me through each fifty-minute game, I'd make sure my pockets contained some extra anti-anxiety meds, which allowed me to function prior to and during the games. I'm almost certain no other coach relied on pharmaceuticals prior to coaching his or her nine year olds.

    But finally, after achieving victory only twice during the regular season, we jelled, winning three games in the season ending tournament and coming in second place, a minor miracle considering our

The View from Under My Desk

inauspicious beginnings.

More than once, depression led me to want to quit this unexpected coaching role, but as I've already said, relationships motivate. There were thirteen girls on the team, each asking questions non-stop while I tried to decide who would play where and making out the batting order, trying to be fair with each girl. On occasion, I had parents in my face, questioning my practice techniques and others offering helpful suggestions. Hauling the equipment, which felt like lead weights, from my car to the playing field was exhausting. I returned home from practices and games almost comatose and needed to lie down on the couch to recover. I ruminated about decisions I'd made, and wondered which parents were mad at me because their daughter didn't get to play in a key position. But seeing the look on my granddaughter's face after she hit a triple kept me going, along with the awareness that she needs activities that offer her relief from the pain she experiences from the divorce. Aware that depression could affect my demeanor at games, I tried to be upbeat with a girl who struck out or made a critical error, offering encouragement and letting her know she made a good effort. I paid a price to coach these girls, but giving back, even in this small way, lifted my spirits—another reminder that doing things for others can help the depression sufferer. My efforts to keep depression at bay during these events took conscious effort and a great deal of willpower. Thankfully I made it through the season.

Brad Anderson

Opening Up, Men and Depression and Being Tedious Beyond Belief

A recent poll found that 54% of the population believes depression to be the result of personal weakness. That figure contributes to the stigma of depression as a character flaw, to be overcome through the sheer force of will. Consider the case of Bob Antonioni.

A cover story in *Newsweek Magazine* in 2007 was titled Men and Depression. It began: *For nearly a decade, while serving as an elected official and working as an attorney, Massachusetts state Sen. Bob Antonioni struggled with depression, although he didn't know it. Most days, he attended Senate meetings and appeared on behalf of clients at the courthouse. But privately, he was irritable and short-tempered, ruminating endlessly over his cases and becoming easily frustrated by small things, like deciding which TV show to watch with his girlfriend. After a morning at the state house, he'd be so exhausted by noon that he'd drive home and collapse on the couch, unable to move for the rest of the day.* Antonioni isn't the only depressive who drives home and collapses on the couch.

After his younger brother committed suicide, Antonioni decided he needed help, so for three years, he secretly met with a therapist, and began taking antidepressants, having his prescriptions filled at a pharmacy 20 miles away. He feared the stigma of being found out. After his chief-of-staff found him crying in his office, he decided he needed to open up about the burden he was trying to keep hidden. He

The View from Under My Desk

started by discussing his depression with friends and family and was later invited to speak at a mental health vigil. After a local reporter wrote about his struggles, he was hailed as a hero by his constituents. Perhaps the stigma is lifting, if ever so slightly. Newsweek concludes its article by noting, *"The result is a hidden epidemic of despair that is destroying marriages, disrupting careers, filling jail cells, clogging emergency rooms and costing society billions of dollars in lost productivity and medical bills. It is also creating a cohort of children who carry the burden of their fathers' pain for the rest of their lives." Newsweek, February 25, 2007.*

"Though he didn't know it" is a key phrase in the case of Bob Antonioni and for many men suffering with depression. Women are much more attuned to their emotional states, and more readily recognize when something is off kilter. They tend to seek help from their family doctors, therapists, and psychiatrists, confiding the symptoms of their malaise and seeking treatment. And as it turns out, twice as many women as men suffer with depression. Men, on the other hand, often miss the warning signs and treat their worsening mood states in a variety of ways, including substance abuse, sexually acting out, gambling to excess, and in some cases, through violence. For anyone, male or female, who suspects depression has insinuated itself in their psyche, google BDI, or Beck Depression Inventory. This self-scoring self-assessment has 21 multiple-choice questions and can quickly give you a reading on your emotional health.

Even before its severity increased and I was

much less depressed, I would be working on the computer in my study and find myself lying on the floor in my closet, with a bathrobe across the bottom of the door to block out any light. Funny how at the time I didn't think this was an odd practice. But being prostrate on the floor in a completely darkened room brought some relief. On a recent Sunday, I spent more time than usual lying on the couch in my basement. I lacked the interest to watch the golf tournament that I'd normally track with obsession. I couldn't have cared less. "Markedly diminished interest or pleasure in all, or almost all, activities most of the day" had kicked in and I didn't care. The DSM has that one right.

Kay Redfield Jamison is the best-selling author of several books on depression, bi-polar disorder and suicide. She's also been a sufferer herself and credits the drug lithium with her survival. Jamison has been CNN's go-to expert whenever a celebrity or other high-profile person shows up with some form of mental illness, just as Dr. Drew is counted on to enlighten us about a celebrity's addiction. I read and reread this passage from her book, *An Unquiet Mind*, as it so deftly describes her experience with depression. *"Depression is awful beyond words or sounds or images; I would not go through an extended one again. It bleeds relationships through suspicion, lack of confidence and self-respect, the inability to enjoy life, to walk or talk or think normally, the exhaustion, the night terrors, the day terrors. There is nothing good to be said for it except that it gives you the experience of how it must be to be old, to be old and sick, to be*

The View from Under My Desk

dying; to be slow of mind; to be lacking in grace, polish, and coordination; to be ugly; to have no belief in the possibilities of life, the pleasures of sex, the exquisiteness of music, or the ability to make yourself and others laugh. Others imply that they know what it is like to be depressed because they have gone through a divorce, lost a job, or broken up with someone. But these experiences carry with them feelings. Depression, instead, is flat, hollow, and unendurable. It is also tiresome. People cannot abide being around you when you are depressed. They might think that they ought to, and they might even try, but you know and they know that you are tedious beyond belief: You're irritable and paranoid and humorless and lifeless and critical and demanding and no reassurance is ever enough. You're frightened and you're frightening, and you're "not at all like yourself but will be soon, but you know you won't.

At a recent family gathering, I fit Redfield Jamison's description of being "tedious beyond belief." Nothing I tried could pull me out of the black hole I'd fallen into. To make matters worse, I was highly aware of my foul mood and its dampening effect on what was to have been a fun day together. In the end, I disappeared into my bedroom in order to save my family from having to work around my gloominess. There had been no failure of will on my part—I was highly motivated to set the tone for a festive holiday gathering. The emotional and physical energy was simply absent that day, and no amount of will power, desire, or inner motivation could jolt me into a state of normalcy. The next day, I sent an email to all the adults who'd been present, apologizing for my behavior and letting them know I didn't want them to believe that I thought my demeanor to be acceptable.

Another SSRI Failure

I recently learned that a new, revised version of *The Noonday Demon: An Atlas of Depression*, from which I've often quoted, had been published. Not much in the revised edition was new to me, but I did read of an antidepressant I hadn't heard of, Brintellix, and I asked my psychiatrist what he thought. Having researched its side effects (nausea, rash, and a list of annoying but seemingly tolerable discomforts), I thought it sounded worth trying. My psychiatrist warned me that the nausea could be severe, mentioned that it was extremely expensive, and told me he could send me some free samples, which I eagerly awaited, wanting to see if a medication did, in fact, exist that could positively alter my mood. He's told me on several occasions that he'd like me to try an SSRI, this drug being in that category, so that made me feel like this was the right thing to do.

It would prove to be the worst experience I've ever had with a psychotropic medication. The first two days on the starter dose of the drug were uneventful. On day three, I experienced some manic symptoms but nothing serious. Day four was the same as the first two days—no side effects. On the

The View from Under My Desk

evening of day four, I took my 5mg starter dose (10-20 mgs being the target dose) and went to bed. The next morning, I awoke much earlier than usual; never a good sign when every day is a fight with fatigue, even with Adderall to bolster my flagging energy levels. I tried going back to sleep to no avail—I was up for the day. I dragged myself out of bed, made breakfast, read the newspaper on the computer, and then felt like I'd been visited by the angel of death.

Depression like I've never felt in my life overtook me. By that time of the morning, I would normally be getting ready for work. Work was the furthest thing from my mind. I made my way to my basement hideaway and curled up in a ball on the couch, something I'd never done prior to starting the day. My mind told me I had to get up and go to work, and after several more minutes of agony, I forced myself up and made my way upstairs. But staying off the couch would be short lived. Once more, I descended the staircase and resumed the fetal position. I began having thoughts of bizarre ways of killing myself, with depression worsening beyond that which I thought possible. It was now about 8:30am, a time I would have been well on my way to work and all I could do was lie there, wanting to die. Finally, I managed to sit up in order to text my psychiatrist. I knew there was nothing he could do to ease the hell I was in, but I felt the need to tell him how horribly wrong this drug was, a drug meant to alleviate, not exacerbate the symptoms of depression. The toll it was taking was beyond what I thought I could bear.

I typed out this text: "Concerns with Brintellix. Day 5 with 5 mg woke up very early today which means I'll be fighting for energy all day. Bigger concern: worst suicidal ideation ever. Depression much worse. Before getting ready for work went downstairs and laid on couch; did this twice before forcing self to get ready. It's early in the morning and I don't know how I'm going to get through the day. My softball team is in the semifinals and I have to be there tonight. Do I just push through and keep taking these and hope it gets better? Nothing extra bad has happened in my life to cause this. Advice?"

Before sending the text, I read it to make sure it said what I wanted to say. I then deleted the suicidal ideation part, not wanting him to commit me to the psych ward. I pushed send and almost immediately he called. He talked non-stop for a long time, acknowledging he had drunk too much coffee, was over caffeinated, hadn't listened to my version of events, and asked what I had to say. My depression was so severe I couldn't even reply. Without knowing about my suicidal thoughts, which I wasn't going to act on, he was handicapped in knowing just how dire my situation was. My best recollection was he advised me to rest, that these effects would be short lived, and to keep taking the drug. I obviously hadn't done a good job at communicating the degree of distress I was in.

The day looked grim. It was 8:30am and I had to go to work, then, depending upon how the softball team performed that evening, would have to coach not one, but two games back to back, all the while needing to be fully functional as I observed the girls play. After a few more minutes of couch time, I did get ready for work, but when I got there, could only lay my head on the desk. Using a great deal of effort and will power, I sent one email. Then I drove home. When I walked in the door, I told my wife what the pills were doing. I had previously told her that I was starting a new antidepressant, and I knew her hopes were high. Having seen me start and then stop one antidepressant after another from intolerable side effects, she impatiently but understandably (to her) told me I had to keep taking them, and to go back to work, which I did with the same result.

Back in the office, I looked up the drug's side effects. I found this statement under the heading **Clinical Worsening and Suicidal Risk**: *"There has been a long-standing concern that antidepressants may have a role in inducing worsening depression and the emergence of suicidality in certain patients during the early phases of treatment."* I made a screenshot of this statement on my phone, intending to send it to both my psychiatrist and my wife, with a comment along the lines of: *"I'm not going to kill myself, but I want you to know this is from the drug's website and my depression is much worse."*
Knowing they could do nothing to lessen the pain, I didn't send the text. I ended up going into work three times that morning, each time leaving after a few minutes of complete inactivity.

Somehow, I made it to 1:30pm. Only three more hours to go before it would be time to pick up my granddaughter for the game. They would be three hours of torture. I did everything I could think of to distract myself from the hell I was in. I filled the car with gas, I called the assistant coach to go over last-minute lineup issues, I went to the library and checked out two John Grisham novels. I texted my boss that I was sick and asked if we could meet the following day. When he didn't text back, paranoia kicked in, since I thought he might have come looking for me and wondered if I were slacking.

    Finally, I drove to my granddaughter's house. When she answered the door, she commented on how early I was. I told her to take her time getting ready, and sat in the car, air conditioning on high, wondering how I was going to get through what would turn out to be two softball games. When she finally emerged from her house, we drove to a deserted ballpark, arriving well before anyone else would show. Since it was a hot day, I didn't want to wear her out by playing catch or having her take batting practice, so we sat in the car, talked, and waited for the team to show up.

    Following our team's unexpected accomplishment of achieving second place in the tournament, I summoned all my energy and announced to the parents there would be a short awards ceremony in the shade on the sidelines. I gave a fittingly enthusiastic speech, talking about how far we had come as a team. I next called each girl by name, asking her to make her way to the front of the crowd where I awarded her with a bright yellow tee shirt the city had provided us for placing second. As I called out each girl's name, I led the parents in a round of applause. Depressed and exhausted as I've ever been, I think I fooled everyone through the sheer force of will.

After dinner with my wife at a restaurant, I forced myself to stay up as long as I could, finally retiring around 9pm, hoping for a better day ahead. It was not to be. After I looked up the half-life of the drug, my hopes for a quick recovery plummeted. The half-life is the amount of time it takes for half the drug to exit the boy. This drug's half life was 66 hours, an eternity which meant that day six would be only slightly better than day five. The next day started with a long meeting with my boss, who mercifully, did most of the talking. I listened, took notes, and nodded a lot. Next, there was a company lunch, and I somehow managed to participate in the festivities celebrating an employee's work anniversary. To cap off the softball season, I'd scheduled a pool party for the girls on the team. I braced myself for the party, frantically running from this task to that to get the pool ready in hopes the girls would have a fun time. The pool party was a success, and after cleaning up, I collapsed into bed.

Day seven would be no better. I once again awoke early, "extreme fatigue" as my companion. It was the first day of the British Open golf tournament and given the time difference between Scotland and the Mountain Time Zone, play at that early hour was being televised. I managed to watch a few minutes of the action before turning off the television and lying on the couch again. The British Open is one of the four major golf tournaments of the year, and I track each one closely. But the fatigue was so overpowering, I checked out and hoped for this hellish drug to exit my system. Once again, I made my way to the office, but was completely non-functional, driving home after realizing I had nothing to give.

I won't elaborate further on the effects of Brintellix–now renamed as Trintellix. The only positive I took away from the experience was to vow never to attempt another antidepressant. I eventually consulted www.askapatient.com to see what others had to say, finding exactly what I expected. For some, it had restored them to sanity. For others, the side effects were intolerable. I take some solace in knowing that my body is eliminating this drug with each passing hour. The anticipation of these pills arriving via FedEx has been replaced by frustration and disappointment and an experience with depression that gave me new renewed motivation to do my due diligence before starting a new medication.

Anhedonia—Sucking the Pleasure Out of Life

I live in the Rocky Mountains, and have access to, as my state of Utah's license plate proudly proclaims, The Greatest Snow on Earth. My parents started me skiing at the age of ten, and I've been an avid aficionado of the sport ever since, always looking forward to the new ski season each fall. However, anhedonia has kicked in. Anhedonia is the term psychologists use to describe one of depression's defining characteristics. It comes from the root, hedonic, as in hedonism, and refers to a person's inability to experience joy and pleasure in activities that once produced these emotions. This year, for the first time, I didn't care about skiing; in fact, it became a chore each time I did manage to get up the energy to go. I'm used to skiing most of the day, but this year I would be ready to leave after a couple of hours and looking forward to departing the resort would bring a sense of relief. After being involved in an activity that brought me pleasure, and even joy on many occasions, it feels like I've lost an old friend. Nothing about skiing changed. The ski resorts didn't change; the snow conditions didn't change; my equipment didn't change; the people I ski with didn't change—I changed. Anhedonia is real.

    Throughout my adult life, I've been passionate about two sports. One is skiing, the other golf. As I mentioned earlier, I played college golf on a scholarship. Don't get me wrong—I was never good enough to even consider playing golf as a career but had enough skill in the sport to enable me to enjoy my time on the course. I got some of my children involved, and we've had many enjoyable outings on the links. Golf is a very demanding and unforgiving sport. To be proficient requires a concerted effort to keep one's game sharp enough to hit enough good shots during a round to make you want to come back and do it again. This requires practice, which involves spending hours on the driving range and putting green.

    I have a friend from high school who made it big in the ice cream business and loves to play in golf scrambles, for which he pays the entry fee, which can be upwards of $5,000. Scrambles are a competitive format where everyone in the foursome hits their shot, then all assemble around the best ball and continue to do so on until the hole is finished. It's a friendly affair, but all of us on the scramble team want to do well. We've even won a couple of tournaments, so our expectations for playing well are high. The last thing I want to do is play poorly and let my teammates down. So I buy a pass to the local driving range and force myself to practice.

    In doing so, I confront two problems: practice is anything but enjoyable—I can't wait until I've hit all the balls in my bucket, and secondly, Adderall, the drug that enables me to get through the day, so over stimulates my body that I lose my rhythm and timing, causing me to tense up in an attempt to over swing, hitting one poor shot after another. Prior to my use of this stimulant, I had a handicap of around 5, which reflected a respectable skill level. Now I don't even maintain a handicap because it would be so high. People who've seen me play the sport in my pre-Adderall days have expressed surprise after witnessing me hit shots akin to a beginner. I soldier on, trying to recapture my old athleticism but ultimately get undone by the drug. So I've gone from a depressed, competent golfer to an over stimulated and slightly less depressed lousy golfer. And anhedonia makes practice a grueling chore to be gotten over with as quickly as possible. Yet I know I have to hold on to some type of hobby and forcing myself to ski and golf is how I engage in these sports.

    How else does this hellish condition show up? As has been mentioned, depression is the

The View from Under My Desk

number one cause of disability worldwide. Just for fun, I recently went online to see if I'd be eligible to qualify for disability and submitted a form. I received a call from a government official, informing me that if I did, in fact, qualify, my monthly payment would be exactly $1,070. That amount, combined with my wife's teacher's salary, would leave us with enough income to cover the basics. That's without the furnace going out, or the car needing major work, or a major dental bill or some other unforeseen and costly expense. The company I work for doesn't include me in their benefits plan, making my wife's job and the medical benefits that go with it indispensable. I'm grateful for every day that allows me to *not* join the ranks of the disabled—I'm good for now. So even though my current job is a far cry in many ways from my position at Covey during the glory days, I'm grateful for the work. I'm also determined to work until I'm stopped cold by this condition—it occasionally takes every ounce of fortitude I can muster to show up. And I'm even grateful for that large, isolating place I call my office. I've already mentioned hardly anyone ever visits, a less than ideal environment for battling depression. I crave contact with other human beings, and this office arrangement is far from ideal in fostering human interaction. But there is that one benefit I mentioned in the introduction for which I'm oddly grateful—the ability to lie on the floor, undetected.

Chapter 22: Wrapping Up and the Role of the Will in Depression

"We must accept finite disappointment, but never lose infinite hope."
Martin Luther King, Jr.

    I believe anyone suffering from depression has to find his or her own unique pathway to relief. Solomon says it this way, *"People are discouraged by the news that every case of depression is different from all others, that what works for one person will fail for the next. But that unwelcome reality is the truth of the matter."* Pg. 482, The NoondayDemon. I don't believe I'll ever be depression free. Part of the solution to finding one's own way through the maze of psychologists, psychiatrists, books, medications, and other purported solutions is persistence. There are caring and competent therapists who can help their clients learn more effective coping strategies and untangle counterproductive thought processes— I just need to find one. The search continues.

    People's reactions to the drug Effexor illustrates the range of experiences people have with anti-depressants. On the website called askapatient.com, people can rate drugs they have used. One 70-year-old woman rated Effexor with a 1, listed depression as her reason for using it, noted side effects as weight gain and sleeplessness, and commented that *"I took this for 12 weeks. I have now spent 10 weeks trying to get off it. One of the antidepressants that you must be weaned off of. No one warned me of this. If you come off too fast you*

The View from Under My Desk

suffer from sweats, dizziness, nausea. It feels like a very bad case of the flu. Never again!" She doesn't mention the number of milligrams in her once a day dose. On the other hand, another poster, a 38-year old woman, rated the same drug as a 5; she takes it for depression, said her side effects were none, and commented, *"Awesome drug. I am SO thankful for it! I'm very fond of it."* She has been using it for one year and takes one dose of 75 milligrams per day. In reading these posts, you can find people who claim the drug in question saved their lives, and you can also read tragic comments by friends and family members who claim the same drug was responsible for a person's suicide.

    I've tried just about every treatment psychiatry has to offer, with the exception of a type of brain surgery known as cingulotomy, perhaps the most radical of ways to rid oneself of the demon. I have taken so many drugs intended to alleviate my melancholy I've forgotten their names. My research showed that antidepressants typically don't approach the success rates shown in clinical trials. According to David Mischoulon, MD, PhD, and associate professor of psychiatry at Johns Hopkins School of Medicine and director of the Woman's Mood Disorders Center, "We have known for many, many years that these antidepressants don't have the kinds of response rates in the real world of practice that they have in those clinical trials that are funded by the industry or by the government." http://www.webmd.com/depression/features/are-antidepressants-effective. My critics would be quick to point out that I've been dealing with only half the equation by not engaging in a concerted effort to work with a talk therapist. I know there are gifted therapists who've done immense good for their clients, lessening depressive symptoms, increasing the quality of life for clients, and preventing suicides, and I in no way want to discourage a depression sufferer from seeking the services of a competent therapist.

To be clear, I am neither a clinician nor a psychiatrist. As a layperson having done a fair amount of reading on the subject, I would never discourage someone from seeking relief from antidepressants since they do work for many, nor would I encourage someone to discontinue their drug regime that's lessening their depression.

If I Could Have a Do-Over

If I could go back to 1998, I would have saved myself tremendous grief if I'd cashed out my Covey stock as soon as the two-year lock up period was over and followed Jackie Burke's advice about being productive and staying off the golf course. Depression would have still been a major factor in my life, but I'm sure that the lack of meaningful work made me more vulnerable.

This next section may seem out of place as it contains four strategies I've recently learned about, all independent of the vagaries of the workplace, which has been the focus of this book. To not share these would be to deprive a depression sufferer of potentially valuable information, and I hope the reader will forgive their placement outside an organizational context.

Depression Fighting Strategy: Look Online

A recent article in the *New York Times* titled *Depressed? Try Therapy Without the Therapist* (June 19, 2015) caught my attention. I've mentioned my lack of success with talk therapy, so I signed up and began this new program called MoodGym. Here's how the Times article begins: *"Elle is a mess. She's actually talented, attractive and good at her job, but she feels like a fraud — convinced that today's the day she'll flunk a test, lose a job, mess up a relationship. Her colleague Moody also sabotages himself. He's a hardworking, nice person, but loses friends because he's grumpy, oversensitive and gets angry for no reason.*

If you suffer from depression or anxiety as Elle and Moody do, spending time with them could help. They are characters in a free online program of cognitive behavioral therapy called MoodGYM, which leads users through quizzes and exercises — therapy without the therapist.

Cognitive behavioral therapy is a commonly used treatment for depression, anxiety and other conditions. With it, the therapist doesn't ask you about your mother — or look at the past at all." The article goes on to point out that cognitive behavioral therapy, which MoodGYM is based on, is the most effective treatment for depression. *"For common mental disorders like anxiety and depression, there is no evidence Internet-based treatment is less effective than face-to-face therapy," according to Pim Cuiijpers, professor of clinical psychology at the Vrije Universiteit Amsterdam and leading researcher on computer C.B.T."* I decided to give it a go, and as I was working my way through the program, I came across this statement about cognitive behavioral therapy, which many therapists claim is the gold standard in treating depression: *"Changing your view about yourself, changing your thoughts about events and changing your view of the future will change the way you feel. This is a really simple idea but highly effective.*

Cognitive Therapy maintains that your emotions are strongly influenced by what you think. Negative emotions are caused by thinking negative (or warped) thoughts. Positive emotions are caused by thinking positive (or unwarped) thoughts." I found this to be a clear-headed analysis of how events and emotions are linked, and I plan to complete my foray into MoodGym. The article does acknowledge the importance of human contact, which could include involving a therapist, but such contact could also be with a peer. One disadvantage with self-guided cognitive behavioral therapy is that people don't stick with it. Another downside to online therapy could occur when a seriously disturbed patient truly does need the face-to-face interactions of a therapist. But overall, this new online system appears to have many advantages, including not having to possess health insurance. People who could not otherwise access therapy can do so simply by logging on to the site. And this free online clinic is available 24/7, so there is no need to go through the often times arduous process of finding a therapist that's right for you, scheduling an appointment, driving to the therapist's office, undergoing multiple visits, and paying for the services rendered.

Depression Fighting Strategy: Exercise If You Can

For me, depression is as much a physical sensation as it is an emotional one. My body feels heavy, each movement requiring an act of the will to move about. I've read countless articles extolling the benefits of exercise for the depressed.

One article in the *New York Times*, *How Exercise May Protect Against Depression*, had this to say, *"Exercise may help to safeguard the mind against depression through previously unknown effects on working muscles, according to a new study involving mice. The findings may have broad implications for anyone whose stress levels threaten to become emotionally overwhelming. Mental health experts have long been aware that even mild, repeated stress can contribute to the development of depression and other mood disorders in animals and people. Scientists have also known that exercise seems to cushion against depression. Working out somehow makes people and animals emotionally resilient, studies have shown."* How Exercise May Protect Against Depression, New York Times, October 1, 2014

I think encouraging the depressed to exercise is wonderful advice, advice that has been proven scientifically. But as my depression has worsened, so has my desire to exercise. If a depressed person can summon the will and the energy to exercise, my hat goes off to them. But the reality is that for most suffering the stagnation of severe depression, the last thing they can do is engage their bodies in strenuous activity. For those struggling to get out of bed in the morning, the thought of donning exercise duds and getting on the treadmill is anathema. I used to exercise regularly; today it's less frequent, although a good week consists of up to three workouts. Perhaps if you're reading this as a sufferer, you can take it as a challenge and follow the advice of those who research the relationship between exercise and depression. You'll feel better about yourself and your body will forgive you once it's recovered.

Depression Fighting Strategy: Mindfulness Meditation

I recently read some blog posts by a psychiatrist on the practice of mindfulness meditation as a treatment for depression. I found this definition in *The Greater Good—The Science of a Meaningful Life:* "Mindfulness means maintaining a moment-by-moment awareness of our thoughts, feelings, bodily sensations, and surrounding environment. Mindfulness also involves acceptance, meaning that we pay attention to our thoughts and feelings without judging them—without believing, for instance, that there's a "right" or "wrong" way to think or feel in a given moment. When we practice mindfulness, our thoughts tune into what we're sensing in the present moment rather than rehashing the past or imagining the future."

http://greatergood.berkeley.edu/topic/mindfulness/definition

On the practice of mindfulness meditation, Forbes weighed in, *"On the list of ways in which meditation appears to benefit the brain, depression treatment may be the latest to gain scientific backing. A new review study in the Journal of the American Medical Association (JAMA) Internal Medicine, finds that mindfulness meditation may rival antidepressants in easing the symptoms of depression. The review is noteworthy for this reason: Its authors combed thousands of earlier studies on meditation, arriving at a small number of randomized clinical trials (the gold standard in science) for use in the analysis.*

Mindfulness meditation may not cure all, the research found, but when it comes to the treatment of depression, anxiety, and pain, the practice may be just as effective as medication." The article goes on to say, *"So when it comes to treating depression, which has a notoriously low treatment success rate, the effect size for meditation in the current study is actually pretty impressive."* Forbes 1/07/2014. A popular TED talk entitled *All It Takes is 10 Mindful Minutes* got over 5 million views. A caveat: the information I read emphasized that future research is needed to demonstrate mindfulness as a clearly useful approach in the treatment of depression. And the miraculous invention of the smartphone with a never-ending plethora of apps doesn't disappoint, as Headspace can be downloaded and guide the user through 10-minute meditation sessions.

Depression Fighting Strategy: Ketamine Infusions

The Treatment Resistant Mood Disorders clinic at the University of Utah has three weapons in its arsenal as it seeks to alleviate the suffering of those who aren't helped by medication and therapy. The clinic offers ECT and transcranial magnetic stimulation (TMS), both of which I've failed. Their third option is one not yet approved by the FDA and not covered by insurance. This extremely expensive treatment is called ketamine infusion. I mentioned ketamine in an earlier chapter and described how ketamine *injections* were of no value. Intrigued by the term *infusion*, I investigated and learned that unlike injecting ketamine directly into my muscles, an infusion consists of inserting an IV into the patient's arm and slowly infusing the anesthetic over a forty-minute time period over several sessions, typically twice weekly for four weeks. At the time I learned of this different method of delivering ketamine, I had met with an ECT doctor to discuss receiving that treatment in a more aggressive form and had scheduled myself to undergo bi-frontal ECT, which came with the promise of increased cognitive impairment and greater memory loss. As the date of my first ECT appointment drew near, Debbi had recently learned about ketamine infusion therapy and was encouraging me to take that route. As I questioned her concerning the pros and cons of the two treatments, I learned that she had been distraught eight years earlier when I underwent ECT. I hadn't known of her distress all those years ago as she explained how unpleasant it was for her to watch me go through twelve rounds of having my brain convulsed. The cognitive impairment and memory loss were upsetting to her and she didn't want to have to see me in that state again, hence her push for ketamine infusions.

With her concerns in mind, I made an appointment with a ketamine infusion psychiatrist at the University and was evaluated for this form of treatment. The doctor explained that their limited experience with this still experimental process was showing great promise, relieving symptoms in up to three quarters of those receiving infusions. He also talked about the cost, and in an almost embarrassed manner explained that the fees for infusions were the primary reason that those in need didn't go forward with this approach. I next had to pass a physical exam, which went smoothly and was set for my first infusion. Debbi and I discussed the cost issue and she made it clear that if this could help me, it was worth the expense.

One requirement the clinic has is that patients are not allowed to drive after treatments, necessitating that I find a driver each time. As I got in the car of a friend who was driving me to my second infusion, he remarked that I appeared significantly different from our previous get together a couple of months prior. He commented that my voice sounded much less depressed, and that I had more life in me. This was consistent with the psychiatrist's evaluation after the fourth treatment when he said that my "affect" had improved. He went on to say that I shouldn't be looking for major improvements, but that the effects would be subtle, that I would take two steps forward and one back. I mentioned to him that I had handled a difficult family situation much more maturely than I would have in the past, yet I wasn't experiencing a lift in my mood. Again, he reassured me using the word subtle, and encouraged me to continue with the treatments.

One definite benefit was noticed after the second infusion, which was that my thoughts of suicide decreased dramatically. This hit me one night as I was lying in bed and I had the thought, "I'm not thinking of killing myself!" I found this as further evidence that decreased suicidal ideation is an outcome that's likely: There is some evidence suggesting that even if an individual's response to ketamine is imperfect or incomplete, it may still be of benefit for certain symptoms of depression. One study (Murrough et al, 2013) reported, "Of particular note, suicidal ideation (SI) rapidly decreased across the total study sample, even among study non-responders. While preliminary, this result suggests that ketamine may exert a unique anti-SI effect even in the absence of a full response and is consistent with previous reports highlighting the potential anti-SI effects of ketamine in depressed populations."

Recipients of ketamine infusions who receive a therapeutic benefit become lifelong patients, as maintenance treatments are required to keep the

The View from Under My Desk

effects in play. That means the costs never end and that I'll need to make the trip to the University at least once a month for as long as I feel the treatments are improving my mental health. I'm cautiously optimistic.

    I mentioned that I didn't find much that was new to me in Solomon's revised book, but I did read about a long-term sufferer who had a course in TMS on the left side of his brain reported pain and no beneficial result. So the doctors switched to the right side of his brain, and he reported the effect was similar to "Ping-Pong balls bouncing off my head." About a year later, this patient's doctor informed him that the machine had been refined and advised him to give it a go one more time, all to no avail. *"I became stupid. I had a hard time following conversations. I'm ten standard deviations down on the memory section of the IQ test. I couldn't follow a sentence. I couldn't make a sentence."* His doctor, obviously going the extra mile to help his patient, contacted researchers at Harvard who were investigating TMS. The Harvard researchers hesitantly suggested trying bi-lateral use of the magnets.

    "So we do the right and then the left a few minutes later," the patient recalled. "I could immediately tell that this was going to work." When last contacted, he was in semi-remission for fourteen months on bilateral TMS. Having gone through TMS on one side of my brain, this discovery gave me a glimmer of hope and a desire to investigate this different application of a procedure I'd undergone if ketamine infusions fail to work their magic.

Brad Anderson

What I Hope to Gain with this Book

Career wise, I try to find satisfaction in small accomplishments, accepting the reality that I'll never create another *Seven Habits of Highly Effective People* program. I practice radical acceptance, although not frequently enough. I continually exercise radically accepting that my life can be worthwhile in spite of the significant financial losses I've incurred. I exercise when I can will myself to do so and avoid berating myself when I can't. And I hold out hope that I can someday find a therapist with the training, insight, personality, and wisdom to help.

Some people who know I'm writing this book have asked me what I hope to gain by this memoir of depression. I definitely wasn't motivated by a desire for catharsis; many of the stories and incidents have resurrected painful memories—and I know there will be those who will likely be offended at my recollection of events. So be it. I haven't intentionally set out to offend anyone. However, I trust my memories, especially the ones communicated in this book since they were so fraught with emotion, and in many cases, the events that occurred during my various places of employment can be validated by others who were present during certain critical incidents I've referred to. My hope in writing this book hinges on my desire to bring this stigmatized disease more fully into the open, showing that this condition so inadequately labeled as depression is real and painful, that those who suffer often seek relief for periods lasting not days or months, or even years, but sometimes decades, that substance abuse is not the answer, and that medications do exist that, while often accompanied by unpleasant side effects, can dampen the mood disorders that afflict so many.

I also hope the reader perceives my never-ending quest to find remedies that work. My first serious attempt to admit I had a problem that required professional help occurred over twenty-five years ago. While my current drug regime provides some relief, it's far from ideal. I find hope in knowing there are highly competent researchers in universities and pharmaceutical companies investigating new drug therapies.

I know there are academics and practitioners developing new forms of talk-based therapies. I'll keep searching. And my failure to find the right therapist should not be interpreted to mean that alternative isn't a valid and valuable process. I've encountered a number of people who've gained invaluable, life-changing insights from their therapists. I've read many accounts of how therapists have helped their clients alleviate suffering. My most fervent hope for someone reading this book is that belief in a brighter future can be re-kindled if it's waned. Even if the only hope at hand is to lie on one's bed until the fog lifts.

This book has been, in part, a memoir, and as such, I have discussed my own trials and travails without distinguishing between the various types of depression other people experience, ranging from mild, to moderate, to severe, where hospitalization may be required. William Styron suffered from this form of depression and found relief only after being hospitalized. No psychiatrist has ever diagnosed me this way, but my own assessment is that I go throughout my days in a state of moderate depression, with severe depression occurring at times from some onerous triggering event. These episodes eventually pass, and I return to a depression that interferes with my ability to achieve the normal mood state I'd love to have. I'm able to function, although my skill in masking my depression waxes and wanes.

The Power of the Will

I ended an earlier chapter by commenting on the attitudes of the vast majority of those who've never suffered from mental illness, who believe that depression is simply the result of a deficiency of the will, and that the solution is to will oneself out of his or her malaise to a brighter, happier, more functional future. I'd like to revisit the concept of the will in the following way. My belief is that there is a factor that can offer hope to even those most debilitated by this disease. That factor is one's will to fight on in the search for relief. In my case, the fight is still raging, but the on-going search to find something, anything, led me to a partial remedy that has increased my functionality and caused a slight lift in mood. Am I happy to have to depend on the chemicals in these pills, with all their noxious side effects, along with the cost and hassle to obtain them? I would give anything to be free of pills of any kind.

Even with the aid of pharmaceuticals, I still

have depression, I'm just a little more enabled to exercise my will. One of depression's most corrosive effects is to sap the will. Depression can crush the will to get out of bed in the morning, to take a shower and get dressed for the day, to go to work (assuming one is fortunate enough to have a job), to fix a leaky faucet, to tackle a stack of unpaid bills, to confront a difficult coworker, to make the next sales call, to take the car in for an oil change, to coach a softball team, to fix a broken printer, to take a grandchild to get a burger, to reach out to a friend, to go to the grocery store, and to perform the never ending list of tasks life thrusts on us that others seem to do as routines requiring little effort. More than once, I've gone to the refrigerator in the morning after pouring myself a bowl of cold cereal to find there's no milk. Facing this situation, people without depressive symptoms simply drive to the supermarket. For me, I have to summon my will to perform this mundane task, and once in the grocery store, become struck by how effortless it is for the other customers there to load up their grocery carts and make their purchases. Why can't I be that way? I've often asked myself.

  In spite of the heaviness depression imposes on the sufferer, the will to put one foot in front of the other is almost always there, recognizing that medications, talk therapy, other treatments, and/or better and stronger connections to others can facilitate its power. In the end, these remedies can facilitate a person's ability to access his or her will. Prior to writing this paragraph, I was lying on the floor of my office, wanting to drive home to lie on the couch, and hoping no one would enter the office to see me prostrate on the ground. Even though I didn't want to, I pushed myself up off the floor, got a soda, sat down at my desk, and started writing. My experience has been that finding effective treatments has been time-consuming, costly, and frustrating. When treatment is successful, or even partially successful, it enables the will to more fully surface and accomplish tasks thought to be forever left undone. And this communicates to the self that one's will, while not at its peak, is still functioning and available to access.

      Depression is painful. Exercising the tiniest amount of will possible can reduce the pain, even in small increments. Last Saturday, I faced a backyard that was a mess. The pool cover needed to be scrubbed down, a job made much easier with two people. I called my son to help, but he didn't pick up. So I did it myself. The chorine feeder for the pool wasn't working and my pool maintenance service would need to be called. Next, the lawn was overgrown from neglect (depression often leads to putting off tasks that pile up) and would need to be gone over with the lawnmower three times. The grass around the sidewalk needed to be cut back. Two years ago, I paid a repair person several thousand dollars to replace the tile in my pool, as it had begun falling out. Hiring him turned out to be a disaster, as large chunks of tile had come loose and were lying on the floor of the pool. Calls, texts and actual letters sent via the post office failed to elicit a response from this contractor. I reluctantly settled on the legal route, making three trips to the courthouse

The View from Under My Desk

to file a claim against him in small claims court, finding the city's website for filing difficult to navigate.

Each of these tasks required me to will myself to do them. They were anything but effortless, including the simple act of calling the pool service. Taking many breaks, I finally finished what I'd set out to accomplish. I looked over the yard with a sense of satisfaction. In hindsight, if all I'd done that day was call the pool service to schedule an appointment, I would have still gotten something done, however insignificant. I now take pleasure in accomplishing the smallest act my will allows. Unrealistic expectations are the death knell of exercising one's will, because they create impossible scenarios that lead to self-defeating self-talk and unhealthy rumination. I have learned to do what my will allows, I pause, and silently express gratitude for the smallest accomplishment my will allows me to summon. As I lie in bed each night, I've made it a practice to reflect on whatever I got done that day. These small wins propel me to tackle whatever lies on the horizon. Consciously considering a task I engaged with, whether I finished it or not, makes me grateful for the will that allowed that to happen.

In winding down, I want to make a hat tip to Dr. Stephen R. Covey by quoting another great poet he inadvertently introduced me to. Way back in 1986, as a video editor and I were approaching the end of Stephen's presentation that would form the backbone of *The Seven Habits* training course, we came across a favorite quotation of Dr. Covey's from a poet I referred to at the beginning of this book, which he used to wrap up his video presentation. Toward the end of T.S. Eliot's poem, Little Gidding, he writes, *"We shall not cease from exploration and the end of all our exploring Will be to arrive where we started and know the place for the first time."* I have to admit that, while certainly lyrical, the meaning of this phrase in the poem was lost on me. I had some sense of its intent, but wasn't as taken by it as the man who spoke the words on videotape. Now, years later, after having endured the depths of depression's hell, Eliot's words resonate in a specific way.

    I started my career exploration in a remote desert in the service of Uncle Sam. For reasons long forgotten, an employee assistance specialist from The Bonneville Power Administration from Portland was on site delivering a seminar on substance abuse. His handout was the pamphlet I referred to earlier in which Dr. Albert Ellis, one of the founders of cognitive behavior therapy, laid out the simple ABCD model. I look back on the tenets in that document and think of all the times I could have used this approach during the next 40 years. I wish I could have a talk with my 23-year-old self. I would grasp him firmly by his shoulders, shake him vigorously, and demand, "Pay attention to this—it will save you a lot of grief!" My 62-year-old self would be desperately hoping that the young, earnest man of the mid 1970's, who was ready to take on the world with little awareness of what that world would entail, would take heed by starting right then to look for opportunities to apply this simple framework, rather than nonchalantly taking note of another

The View from Under My Desk

academic model. Would it have saved me from the later ravages of depression? No. But it could have lessened the pain of the inevitable setbacks life presents to each of us. Depressives have a default belief system about the adverse activating events of their lives. That belief system ties directly to Seligman's notions of the persistence, permanence and personalization of challenging circumstances. Ellis and his colleagues gave us a way of confronting the default, thereby truncating the inevitable spiral into despair. I hope to become more effective in disputing the irrational beliefs that so often accompany the negative events I encounter.

Depression by its nature causes self-absorption, an obsession with one's own misery. This focus can become tiresome to those in the depressive's sphere and causes the sufferer to be out of tune with the needs of others, whether those needs are physical, mental, emotional, or spiritual. If we're able to recognize that our emotional pain is causing pain for those around us, that awareness can cause us to stop concentrating so hard on ourselves and instead, become more attuned to how other people are feeling Earlier, I referred to Dr. Gabor Maté's research in addiction and speculated that infant brain development could be a factor in setting the stage for depression. Maté discusses this idea of attunement and argues that one risk factor for addiction is "proximate separation" or the idea that a parent can be in close proximity to his or her child but be completely oblivious to that child's needs—out of tune, as it were. The obsession of staring at one's smart phone is a classic example of proximate separation, as a parent's sole focus is on whatever the device is offering up as a distraction to caring for and nurturing a child. Depression can lead to proximate separation; much like a smart phone but without the thrill of checking out how many likes one's latest Facebook post garnered.

Knowing how tiresome it is to hear me verbalize my depressed mood, I try to avoid mentioning the feelings that accompany depression to those closest to me—they already know. To illustrate, I mentioned in an earlier chapter how I'd love to have the energy and persistence to plan and hold a family reunion. Since writing of that wish, I actually got the ball rolling, emailing all my children and settling on a date. I was anxious about this first-time event in my family for several weeks leading up to it. My wife and kids pitched in with ideas, and miracle of miracles, we actually pulled it off. All the adults were on the same page, wanting to create a happy and memorable event for all twenty-three of us. During our three days together, I didn't talk to anyone about depression. However, I did collapse into bed each night, sometimes forgoing an activity here and there. But for the most part, I managed to hold it together, trying to ensure the best experience possible given the diversity of ages, interests, and temperaments.

Service Revisited

On a recent summer Sunday, Debbi and I spent an unusually quiet day at home, as children and grandchildren who usually come for dinner were

The View from Under My Desk

doing other things. That afternoon, I found myself in the bedroom watching a guilty pleasure on Netflix– Nurse Jackie. A twenty year-veteran as a highly competent ER nurse in midtown Manhattan, Nurse Jackie is also an opiate addict, scoring her drugs in creative and unusual ways, including sleeping with the hospital's pharmacist during work hours. Jackie's husband eventually discovers her secrets and files for divorce, gaining custody of their two young daughters. Jackie loses everything, including her nursing license. As I binge watched these highly uplifting and inspiring episodes of the good nurse, Debbi was in the kitchen, and unbeknownst to me, was baking her heart out. That evening, we set out to deliver several small loaves of zucchini bread to elderly neighbors, some ailing and some just to be thoughtful. Debbi has a soft spot in her heart for these aging friends, and she frequently performs small acts of kindness toward them. One of the deliveries went to an 83-year-old woman who had fallen in her basement when attempting to reach something overhead. She'd suffered a concussion and cracked her tailbone. Another neighbor is in his mid-80's and is recuperating from brain surgery. Each small token was accepted with great enthusiasm and warmth. I know it lifted Debbi's spirits to have performed these selfless acts of service. I could take no credit—these were the products of my wife's efforts—all I did was drive the car and converse during the deliveries.

    The experience left me thinking of all the times I'd fired up my John Deere riding mower— which I'd converted into a snowplow—and hit the neighbors' driveways, clearing snow from that day's storm for multiple aging couples and widows living nearby. As I'd go from one driveway to the next, I'd often be hailed with a friendly thank you. However, due to global warming or some other factor influencing the weather, the past few winters have brought few storms with enough snow to warrant employing the plow. Dropping off those small loaves made me reflect on the last time I'd inconvenienced myself for another's sake with no thought of reward as I'd done with all those cleared driveways and sidewalks.

    I thought about how I'd spent *my* day and wondered whatever happened to that person who looked for opportunities to help others. I wondered what happened to the guy who used to hang out with a bunch of second graders during their lunch period and organize baseball games. I wondered about what happened to the guy who, witnessing an underprivileged child's peers mocking his tattered shoes, drove to the local department store and returned with a pair of the coolest sneakers of the day. I wondered what happened to the guy who helped college students struggling with mental illness receive competent treatment by connecting them with therapists I'd vetted. And in the end, I wondered what happened to the guy who eschewed an idle weekend in favor of doing something for someone's benefit. Making those deliveries sobered me. I know I'm not that same guy today, but within the limits of what I *can* do, I can do something other than wiling away the hours until it's time to turn in. Marian Wright Edelman, an American activist for the rights of children, summed up my feelings with this quote, *"Service is the rent we pay for being. It is the very purpose of life, and not something you do in your spare time."* I've used this phrase before, and I use it again: *Within the limits depression imposes*, performing small acts of kindness is one of the best antidotes I know for battling the noonday demon. This short anecdote about zucchini bread demonstrates how the act of serving others can be therapeutic. Over time, I'd lost the benefit of getting outside my inner world of annoying and sometimes debilitating pain and doing *something* for *someone*.

Wisdom from Tennyson

As I conclude, I want to share an experience I had while driving my family from one job to the next. My family of four departed our beloved home and friends in Eugene, Oregon on August 15, 1980 in our two-door Toyota Corolla, sans air conditioning, bound for the excitement of the Silicon Valley. This was the wrong time of year to be driving through Redding, California at mid-day, with temperatures hovering around 110 degrees. It was a draining experience, leaving behind a job that I'd flourished in, along with some dear friends whom we weren't likely to be seeing much of in the future. The heat only added to our misery. By the time we reached San Francisco, Debbi and the two kids were asleep, and I was trying to find something on the radio to keep me awake. What I found on that radio station suddenly jolted me out of any fatigue and sadness I'd been feeling. I'd come upon the 1980

Democratic National Convention, and not being particularly interested in politics, was about to search for a rock station.

But then I heard it—the unmistakable voice of Ted Kennedy delivering his concession speech to Jimmy Carter. Kennedy was quoting from Lord Alfred Tennyson's famous poem, Ulysses, and I'd have no idea how his words would inspire me thirty-five years later. Kennedy introduced his Tennyson quotation by saying it had held special meaning for his brothers. I gave up any thought of finding a top 40 station, and drove on, mesmerized by Tennyson's gift in describing the power of the will. His eloquence far outstrips my meager attempt to highlight its place in our lives, particularly for those dealing with depression: *"I am a part of all that I have met...How dull it is to make an end. To rust unburnish'd, not to shine in use! ...Tho' much is taken, much abides, and tho' we are not now that strength which in old days mov'd earth and heaven, that which we are, we are: One equal temper of heroic hearts, Made weak by time and fate, but strong in will; to seek, to find, and not to yield."* I've since searched "Ted Kennedy 1980" on YouTube, reminiscing on this long-ago memory and attaining strength from Kennedy's delivery of the great poet's words. Each new day presents an opportunity to avoid yielding.

    My career has spanned a diverse number or organizations, including a federal agency, two Fortune 50 companies, and small to mid-sized consulting firms. I've had jobs I've loved and jobs I've loathed. I've been an executive with the budget and autonomy to travel the world, garnering awards and accolades at gatherings like the New York Film Festival, and not too long ago, have been reduced to an $8 an hour underling in a part time, seasonal gig fitting children with ski gear. I've also spent time among the ranks of the unemployed and underemployed. I've made the mistake of investing too much of my self-worth into certain jobs. The ideas I've shared throughout this book are offered as options, to be applied within the limits a depressive is struggling with. Not all are possible to implement. But that doesn't mean options don't exist. There is no one-size-fits-all approach for a depressed person to exist within the demands of the modern organization. We can learn skills, strategies, tactics—call them what you will—to survive (and at times, even thrive)—in our own, unique organizational worlds. If I can do it, anyone can.

Though depression is a weakening experience and deprives the sufferer of capacities once taken for granted, the will, if able to be exercised through medication and/or therapy, strengthens, it gives us the ability to put off yielding, if only for a short time. My hope is that anyone reading this who suffers from depression gains a greater capacity to exercise his or her will. If that can occur, then exposing my own battles with the demon of depression will have been worth the effort.

References

Chapter 1
(http://columbiadailyherald.com/sections/opinion/columns/suicide-cycle-'april-cruelest-month'.html

CPSIA information can be obtained
at www.ICGtesting.com
Printed in the USA
LVHW011353230520
656343LV00005B/282